I0199199

PRAISE FOR
Staying Together

Chapter after chapter, the Prokopchaks hit on the subjects that couples are facing today. I hear about issues like insecurity, healthy boundaries, finances, and sexual struggles all the time. Steve and Mary's personal life stories from real life couples provide helpful solutions for any marriage.

MARK GUNGOR
Author of *Laugh Your Way to a Better Marriage*
www.markgungor.com

If you want a good marriage to be better, or a struggling marriage to be rescued, this book is for you. If you want to understand more about your spouse, yourself, and the divinely planned union called marriage, this book is for you. If you want to be equipped to help others who desire to enrich their marriage relationship, this book is for you.

Steve and Mary Prokopchak, authors of the widely acclaimed pre-marital counseling manual, *Called Together,* have once again provided a must-have resource for couples and counselors alike. Based on real-life questions and real-life challenges, Steve and Mary skillfully and lovingly provide tools that, when utilized, can add strength to every couple's life together. *Staying Together* is straightforward and uncompromising, based on clear biblical guidelines that are made practical and understandable.

IBRAHIM and DIANE OMONDI
Directors, DOVE Africa

Steve and Mary Prokopchak's latest book; *Staying Together,* is an excellent read for every married couple. In fact, chapter five, Moving Beyond Our Histories in which "memory minefields" are dealt with is worth the price of the entire book. The Prokopchaks have personally helped hundreds of couples in their marriage relationships through teaching, pre- and postmarital and marital counseling. This book incorporates their many years of practical marriage principles and tools that will help you take your marriage to the next level. We highly recommend this book!

LARRY and LaVERNE KREIDER
Authors and International Director of DOVE International

Are you serious? Another book on marriage? Well, if you *are* serious—I mean truly serious about building a marriage that will last, that will "Stay Together," then this book is for you. As a marriage and family therapist and author, I appreciate the insights that Steve and Mary Prokopchak bring to the marriage discussion. They don't just present a quick and easy read—they call you to action. Their penetrating discussion questions will force you to dig deep and closely examine what you and your marriage are made of. And their helpful worksheets will provide you with the tools that can help move you toward health in your relationship. So, if you are serious—then I encourage you and your spouse to camp out in in the pages of this book.

BARRY D. HAM, PH.D., LMFT
Author of *Unstuck: Escaping the Rut of a Lifeless Marriage*

Steve and Mary Prokopchak continually serve the body of Christ not only with their profound teaching on marriage but also in being a true example of a godly couple that others can emulate. The revelation, knowledge, and expertise they have on the topic of marriage are phenomenal and much needed in today's confused world. Every page of this book gives deep understanding on God's image of family and marriage. It's very practical and a must read for anyone who wants to succeed in their marriage. Be prepared to be challenged!

DANAIL TENEV
Radio talk show host
Ask Danny Tanev
Sliven, Bulgaria

Staying Together is both practical and relatable, but most of all, it is biblical. These pages are filled with marriage nuggets every reader will discover for themselves. From the bedroom to the budget, you will finally discover a marriage book actually about marriage. With probing questions to answer and loving solutions offered, this book hits the mark every time. We not only enthusiastically endorse but highly recommend this creative book by Steve and Mary Prokopchak.

Great job, Steve and Mary.

PAUL and BILLIE KAYE TSIKA
Get Married-Stay Married

STAYING
together
Marriage: A Lifelong Affair

STEVE & MARY
PROKOPCHAK

© Copyright 2017–Steve and Mary Prokopchak

All rights reserved. This book is protected by the copyright laws of the United States of America. This book may not be copied or reprinted for commercial gain or profit. The use of short quotations or occasional page copying for personal or group study is permitted and encouraged. Permission will be granted upon request. Unless otherwise identified, Scripture quotations are taken from the HOLY BIBLE, NEW INTERNATIONAL VERSION®, Copyright © 1973, 1978, 1984 International Bible Society. Used by permission of Zondervan. All rights reserved. Scripture quotations marked NLT are taken from the Holy Bible, New Living Translation, copyright 1996, 2004. Used by permission of Tyndale House Publishers, Wheaton, Illinois 60189. All rights reserved. Scripture quotations marked NKJV are taken from the New King James Version. Copyright © 1982 by Thomas Nelson, Inc. Used by permission. All rights reserved. All emphasis within Scripture quotations is the author's own. Please note that Destiny Image's publishing style capitalizes certain pronouns in Scripture that refer to the Father, Son, and Holy Spirit, and may differ from some publishers' styles.

DESTINY IMAGE® PUBLISHERS, INC.

P.O. Box 310, Shippensburg, PA 17257-0310

"Promoting Inspired Lives."

This book and all other Destiny Image and Destiny Image Fiction books are available at Christian bookstores and distributors worldwide.

Cover design by Eileen Rockwell
Interior design by Terry Clifton

For more information on foreign distributors, call 717-532-3040.

Reach us on the Internet: www.destinyimage.com.

ISBN 13 TP: 978-0-7684-1490-5
ISBN 13 eBook: 978-0-7684-1491-2
ISBN 13 HC: 978-0-7684-1638-1
ISBN 13 LP: 978-0-7684-1639-8

For Worldwide Distribution, Printed in the U.S.A.

1 2 3 4 5 6 7 8 / 21 20 19 18 17

DEDICATION

We desire to dedicate this book to the many couples we have mentored in marriage because it is our heart they not only stay together but also become even more committed to one another. We wish to thank those who took the time to respond to questionnaires and those who read selected chapters of this text and gave us their feedback in an attempt to create a different kind of marriage book. Our special thanks to our daughter, Brooke, who gave hours of her time and talent to edit the book in its entirety. Thank you, Brooke; we are so pleased that your degree in writing directly benefited this book. Thanks to Destiny Image Publishers for believing in our desire to see marriages strengthened and for publishing this book. And thank You, Father, for Your creative act of this thing we call marriage.

CONTENTS

Introduction..................................11

Chapter One   The "Me" in Us 17

Chapter Two   The Fear and Insecurity Found in Us 39

Chapter Three The "One" of Us 55

Chapter Four   Healthy Boundaries for a
               Healthy Relationship 79

Chapter Five   Moving Beyond Our Histories 93

Chapter Six   Marriage Has a Mission..................... 107

Chapter Seven Fighting and Arguing or Praying
               and Agreeing 129

Chapter Eight Putting Your Money Where Your Value Is.... 141

Chapter Nine   Rebuilding After Loss....................... 163

Chapter Ten   Staying True............................... 175

Chapter Eleven Going Under Cover(s) 189

Chapter Twelve Intimate Conversations 203

Chapter Thirteen The Six Most Important Words.............. 215

Appendix A   Pornography and Sexual Addiction
               Resource List.............................. 223

Appendix B   Annual Marriage Evaluation and
               Vision Retreat 227

Appendix C   The Forgiveness Process..................... 231

INTRODUCTION

After we speak those wonderful words, "I do," we begin to realize that marriage requires a concerted effort on the part of two committed persons. We discover that life is not about changing others to meet our own needs but about changing ourselves to meet the need of others. Our first book, *Called Together*, was about helping to properly prepare couples for marriage, as well as providing two major post-marital check-ups within the first year of marriage. This book, *Staying Together*, goes beyond that first year and builds on the same principles of a lifelong marriage commitment. After 40 years of marriage, we have discovered that the only place you can have it your way is at a famous fast-food burger chain. And even then, they often get your order wrong.

Life is full of imperfection; those of you who felt that your marriage would be a perfect union, well, now we understand why you're holding this book. In the event that marriage has become laborious, if it becomes what you do and not why you do it, you might have lost some vision for your marriage. There are times that we choose to do the work, but that work should eventually give birth to life, love, service, and desire.

Staying Together is for those of you who are willing to contend for a stronger marriage and for those of you who simply desire to draw closer to one another. It is especially for those of you who see your marriage vows as threatened. The exercises and questions found herein are those that we have asked hundreds of people and we wish someone had asked us along the way. While our marriage is certainly not perfect, it is one in which we have continually searched for answers from the Author of marriage. If we have gained any wisdom from our years of marriage, we want to pass it on to you.

Marriage was God's idea from the very beginning; it predates Christianity by thousands of years. While all religions of the world marry, many do not emphasize, as Christianity does, the sacredness of this institution—one that begins with a vow made before the Lord Himself. Marriage is one of those areas of life that is not to be endured as one endures a mundane job; it is to be embraced with every part of our being. Love is more than a season of life or a short-lived feeling. Love is an act of commitment for a lifetime, with or without the butterflies.

Once, when Jesus was asked about divorce, He quoted the Old Testament, reminding His listeners that the Creator of marriage said the man and woman would become one flesh and that if God was joining them together, man was not to separate them. Divorce was not a part of creation; it was a consequence of the fall of man. While not every divorce is sinful, it is the result of humanity's sinful, selfish nature wanting life its own way and not God's way. For those of you who have suffered through a divorce, we do not condemn you; we admire you for pursuing God's plan for marriage. Because God is the source of marriage, and because He is never depleted, He will always have more for you and your marriage.

THIS BOOK HAS BEEN BUILT UPON REAL-LIFE REQUESTS

Several years ago we conducted a survey in which we asked, "If you and your spouse could read through a workbook on marriage, what content would you desire to have included and what would be your most important questions to be confronted/dealt with?" The following is a sampling of the many responses we received and consequently what this book has been built upon.

- We need advice on how to effectively make decisions when there is a difference of opinion.

- What should our sexual expectations be; what is holy and what is good?

- When should we consider consulting a marriage counselor?

- Financial budgeting and living within alignment with our money is our concern.

- How do we reevaluate our roles and practical duties?

- Alignment help with our personal family values would be a key for us.

- We would like help with our marriage mission and purpose.

- It is said that love is not just a feeling but also a decision. What does that mean?

- What are the things within marriage that can help us to grow security and move away from insecurity?

- How can we both be happy at home without constant outside entertainment?

- Confronting the wrong priority of self-esteem attempts and how I/we look to one another for validation.

- Practical help to *not* speak the "D" word—divorce.

- Hearing each other's heart in communication and not just the words.

- How do we forgive rather than attempting to justify our attitude toward being right?

- Should our goal be endeavoring to bring happiness to each other, or…?

- When and how do we talk about counseling simply for a marriage tune-up?

- What is the best way to discuss what isn't right in our marriage?

- Why does it feel like I am the only one changing here?

- How do we respond to criticism that we think is unfair?

- Help! I get so defensive. If we are one, how do I stay open and not allow things to build up?

- How do we get on the same team, all the time?

- Am I just to submit to my husband's wishes, plans, and decisions? When do I as his wife have a say?

- How do I convince her that I am listening most of the time?

- How do we keep our marriage a priority when life pulls us away from one another?

- What do I do with my unmet expectations?

We will address these concerns and more. We pray that this resource evokes positive change in you, thereby causing change for the good in your call and mission together in marriage.

WAYS TO USE THIS BOOK

You can walk through this material as a couple, strengthening your relationship. You can also walk through this material with the help of another couple in a mentoring relationship (as the authors, we feel this is the best way to utilize this book). If you are contending for your marriage alone (meaning without your spouse), then the contents and the exercises of *Staying Together* can be of significant help to you. In addition, you could study the book with an accountability group. The answers from other couples are likely to differ from your own, providing broader insight and perspective to everyone involved.

This material is meant to be interactive. As the authors, we desire you to first interact with your heavenly Father as you consider the challenges of the following pages. Second, keep facing the reality of self-confrontation toward personal change. Third, interact with your spouse by discussing each exercise together. Keep open dialogue and practice hearing one another's heart and not just one another's words. Remember that working through difficulties rather than avoiding them strengthens relationships. Feel free to write down your answers, keep a document on your computer of your answers, or simply discuss them out loud with each other.

Take this opportunity to have fun working together, while at the same time experiencing life-giving responses. Consider taking an exercise or two with you on a date or go away for a weekend and work through several chapters. Do whatever it takes to complete this manual and receive everything you can from it.

Chapter One

THE "ME" IN US

In trying to get our own way, we should
remember that kisses are sweeter than whine.
—AUTHOR UNKNOWN

The heart has its reasons of which reason knows nothing.
—BLAISE PASCAL, *Penées*, 1670

We live in a consumer-oriented society. We can obtain almost anything we desire, and we can have it our way, in our color, in our price range. If it doesn't fit, we can return it. If it breaks, we can replace it. We can call toll-free numbers, complain to our boss, or even hire a lawyer if we are dissatisfied. I (Steve) once had a briefcase on which the handle fell apart. It can be pretty tough to carry a briefcase without a handle, so I contacted the company directly. The customer service representative was very apologetic. She asked for the model number of the briefcase and said she would have a replacement sent to my door, at no cost, no questions asked! Literally the next day there was a box at my door with a brand-new briefcase in it. As a consumer, this company won me over.

Marriage, however, is not for the consumer; marriage is for the committed. Consumerism can spoil us. What happens when we bring consumerism into our marriages? We might expect to have everything our way. We might expect to have our needs met first. We might even expect our spouse to act like a customer service representative, bending over backward to win us over. We might expect a kind, cheery, or calm response to all of our selfish questions and requests. And because the customer is always right, if we act as customers in our marriages we feel perpetually justified.

After years of counseling and speaking all over the world, hearing story after story from many different couples, we have come to realize that most social scientists have missed the mark when it comes to identifying the primary cause of marriage breakup. While finances play a part, as do compatibility and sexual issues, these are all secondary to the primary reason—selfishness. When we become a consumer in our marriage, we become selfish and frequently used to getting what we want.

One time in a marriage counseling session, a husband responded, "I give her whatever she wants. She doesn't work outside the home. She has a car. All I ask is that she..." That sentence could be finished with any number of things—get up and cook me breakfast, give me a back rub and listen to me when I come home from work, balance the checkbook, run the entire household, cook delicious meals, always be available for sex. You get the picture. The spirit of consumerism says, "I give to my spouse, therefore, I expect a certain return." If you're looking for a specific return, then you are looking for an investment and not a committed marriage relationship.

LEVELS OF COMMITMENT WITHIN MARRIAGE

First, we must be committed to God. Our commitment to God must override our commitment to everyone and everything else. First Kings 8:61 says, "But your hearts must be fully committed to the Lord our God, to live by his decrees and obey his commands." When Jesus was asked what the greatest commandment was, He replied that we were to "Love the Lord [our] God with all [our] heart and with all

[our] soul and with all [our] mind" (Matt. 22:37). Love God first. This means His will for us should supersede our will.

Second, we must be committed to our spouse. In committing to one another in marriage, we commit to putting the needs of our spouse before our needs. Jesus once said that the greatest in the Kingdom of Heaven was first a servant. Who is the greatest servant in your household?

Early on in our marriage, we attempted to counsel another young married couple in which the husband was addicted to drugs. His need to get high was his number-one priority in life. Although he loved his wife, she was not as important to him as the drugs he craved. As he destroyed himself, he also destroyed his marriage.

We must also be committed at this same level to ourselves. This is not meant to sound selfish, but in Matthew 22:38 Jesus said that we are to love our neighbor as our self. If we do not have a proper, God-given, and healthy self-image, if we lack "self-love," we will not know how to love another, especially our spouse, who is our closest neighbor.

For example, if, as a spouse, I decide to no longer take care of my teeth, my hair, or care about my weight, then I do not properly love my marriage partner. And if I stop caring about my spiritual self, I will have a direct effect upon my spouse who needs me to love God more than I love her or him. According to the words of Jesus, to not care for myself is the same as not caring for my life mate.

Mary and I were traveling in order to meet with a leadership couple that was experiencing a challenging time in their personal lives. As they began to describe what was happening and how they were feeling, the wife in a rather subdued manner looked straight at me while speaking these words, "I'm done. I'm done trying to please everyone. I'm done trying to diet. I'm done trying to lose weight and use exercise equipment that I just abhor. I am going to eat what I want, do what I want, and not worry about it any longer."

As she spoke, something began to arise within me that I just knew was not from my mind but from my spirit. I looked straight back at her eye to eye and said, "You do realize that what you are telling us is that you are done obeying God's command to care for and to love yourself. You are telling me that your husband and your children and those whom you lead are not worth loving because you are not worth loving. In not taking care of yourself, you are not taking care of those whom you love or will love in the future."

She stared at me and was a bit startled by my direct response. The next day she told me that she was convicted by those words and after repenting made a decision to make the necessary changes in her life. She said she wants to love others as she knows she is loved.

Third, we must be committed to our family. If something happens to one of our children while we are at work, most of us will leave and care for our child. They should have a higher priority to us than our jobs. That being said, our commitment to our spouse must come even before our commitment to our children. This is a vital concept to adopt so that the marriage remains intact after the children are raised. Far too often we have observed couples that have poured their lives into their children or grandchildren and left their marriage to fend for itself. We have seen wonderful mothers get so caught up in mothering that their husbands are left feeling very alone. While children do not raise themselves, marriages cannot be put on hold until the kids are grown. When the children or grandchildren become a higher priority than the marriage itself, the spouses will one day wake up separated physically and emotionally. Do not allow such a devastating separation to occur to you or your marriage.

One long weekend a number of years ago, Steve and I (Mary) were staying with a pastor and his wife where we were speaking. Throughout the weekend we noticed little things in their marriage, and one evening the wife spoke up and said to us, "We have separate bedrooms." We asked them if they desired to talk about it and she began to disclose how the church had become a higher priority to her husband than she and the children. After years of this, the wife finally went back to her teaching career in order to provide for the household and they became all the more distant as a couple.

First they separated emotionally, then financially, then spiritually, then physically, and finally they lived a life of complete divorce minus the paperwork within the same house. The depth of their wounds and the constant pain they lived in was indescribable. To think that it all started with priorities out of alignment.

Finally, commitment to our jobs and local churches, as well as to community efforts and hobbies, is afforded the next level of priority in our lives. These areas, while important, are secondary to the marriage and family. Community action is great, as is running for a local political office or rebuilding a neighbor's old car, but never are these of higher priority than your first obligation—your "community" at home. Our life priorities and levels of commitment speak far louder than our words. When we are in proper alignment with God's priorities for our marriage and family, we will find deeper peace and depth of relationship. This is the type of relationship that God created us for.

Be honest—list your top five priorities in life as they currently are, and not as you would like them to be.

1. _____

2. _____

3. _____

4. _____

5. _____

Who or what comes first as you take a candid self-assessment? A consumer-oriented society will list *self* as its first priority. But this is not the case with God's desire for our lives or His order for our marriages. Discuss your answers as you consider the following questions about consumerism in marriage:

1. If I assess myself honestly, what consumerism am I guilty of within my marriage?

2. What do I need to change in order to not live like a customer in my marriage?

3. How can I reorganize my priorities if they are not aligned with God's priorities?

4. In what areas of marriage do I struggle with selfish ambition?

Continuing your personal assessment, complete the following statements with what first comes to mind. Do these exercises separately from one another and then come together at a later time and discuss what you discovered about yourself. To go more in-depth you can also take the time to share how some of your qualities as well as some of your weak areas interface with one another.

ASSESS ME (WIFE)

1. I see myself as

_____

_____

_____

2. A word that would best describe me is

_____

3. To me, success in life means

_____

_____

_____

4. My strongest quality is

_____

_____

_____

5. One of my weaknesses is

_____

_____

_____

6. My spouse views me as

_____

_____

_____

7. I become quiet when

_____

8. When my spouse has a different opinion than I do, my reaction is to

9. My feelings tend to be hurt when

10. I feel guilty when

11. I worry when

12. I feel accepted by my spouse when

13. What makes me feel inadequate is

14. I feel depressed when

_____

_____

_____

15. I receive pleasure from

_____

_____

_____

16. I am disappointed when

_____

_____

_____

17. Some of my gifts include

_____

_____

_____

18. My self-confidence falters when

_____

_____

_____

19. I get defensive when

_____

_____

_____

20. Something that makes me laugh is

_____

21. I get angry when

22. When angry with my spouse, I tend to

23. I receive great satisfaction from

24. I feel trapped when

25. I am afraid when

26. I feel insecure when

27. I feel most secure when

_____

_____

_____

28. I feel selfish when

_____

_____

_____

29. An area of my life I desire to change is

_____

_____

_____

30. What I fear the most is

_____

_____

_____

ASSESS ME (HUSBAND)

1. I see myself as

_____

_____

_____

2. A word that would best describe me is

_____

3. To me, success in life means

_____

_____

_____

4. My strongest quality is

_____

_____

_____

5. One of my weaknesses is

_____

_____

_____

6. My spouse views me as

_____

_____

_____

7. I become quiet when

_____

8. When my spouse has a different opinion than I do, my reaction is to

9. My feelings tend to be hurt when

10. I feel guilty when

11. I worry when

12. I feel accepted by my spouse when

13. What makes me feel inadequate is

14. I feel depressed when

_____

_____

_____

15. I receive pleasure from

_____

_____

_____

16. I am disappointed when

_____

_____

_____

17. Some of my gifts include

_____

_____

_____

18. My self-confidence falters when

_____

_____

_____

19. I get defensive when

_____

_____

_____

20. Something that makes me laugh is

_____

_____

_____

21. I get angry when

_____

_____

_____

22. When angry with my spouse, I tend to

_____

_____

_____

23. I receive great satisfaction from

_____

_____

_____

24. I feel trapped when

_____

_____

_____

25. I am afraid when

_____

_____

_____

26. I feel insecure when

_____

_____

_____

27. I feel most secure when

_____

_____

_____

28. I feel selfish when

_____

_____

_____

29. An area of my life I desire to change is

_____

_____

_____

30. What I fear the most is

_____

_____

_____

Separately, each of you should complete the following statements concerning your spiritual life. Once finished, consider sharing your responses with each other to see if you can discover something you did not know about your spouse. Consider taking a moment to pray together for spiritual growth individually and as a couple.

SPIRITUAL OVERVIEW (WIFE)

1. My personal relationship with Jesus is

_____

_____

_____

2. My definition of sin is

_____

_____

_____

3. Describe how you deal with sin:

_____

_____

_____

4. In what ways do you feel that Jesus is the Lord of your life? (Please elaborate.)

_____

_____

_____

_____

_____

_____

5. As a believer, what is your experience with the Holy Spirit?

_____
_____
_____

6. Describe your prayer life (Where? When? Why? etc.):

_____
_____
_____

7. I read the Bible (When? For what reasons? etc.):

_____
_____
_____

8. My personal commitment to attending a church (i.e., a body of believers) is (How often? For what reasons?)

_____
_____
_____

9. My understanding of God is

_____
_____
_____

10. In a spiritual sense, marriage solves the following problems:

_____
_____
_____
_____

11. In a spiritual sense, marriage creates the following problems:

_____

_____

_____

_____

12. I would like to make the following change(s) in my spiritual life:

_____

_____

_____

_____

_____

_____

_____

_____

_____

SPIRITUAL OVERVIEW (HUSBAND)

1. My personal relationship with Jesus is

_____

_____

_____

2. My definition of sin is

_____

_____

_____

3. Describe how you deal with sin:

_____

_____

_____

4. In what ways do you feel that Jesus is the Lord of your life? (Please elaborate.)

_____

_____

_____

_____

_____

_____

_____

5. As a believer, what is your experience with the Holy Spirit?

_____

_____

_____

6.   Describe your prayer life (Where? When? Why? etc.):

_____

_____

_____

7.   I read the Bible (When? For what reasons? etc.):

_____

_____

_____

8.   My personal commitment to attending a church (i.e., a body of believers) is (How often? For what reasons?)

_____

_____

_____

9.   My understanding of God is

_____

_____

_____

10. In a spiritual sense, marriage solves the following problems:

_____

_____

_____

_____

11. In a spiritual sense, marriage creates the following problems:

_____

_____

_____

12. I would like to make the following change(s) in my spiritual life:

_____

_____

_____

    Commitment to not be a consumer in our marriage means facing our own self-centeredness. It means taking responsibility for the "me" in us and being willing to take personal responsibility for change.

Chapter Two

THE FEAR AND INSECURITY FOUND IN US

*I still have pretty much the same fears I had as a
kid. I'm not sure I'd want to give them up; a lot
of these insecurities fuel the movies I make.*
—STEVEN SPIELBERG

*I have the show because I'm insecure. It's
my insecurity that makes me want to be a
comic that makes me need the audience.*
—RAY ROMANO

Who we were as a single person is who we brought into the marriage. We brought all of our history, our family of origin, our
securities and insecurities, our gifts and talents, and our individual
likes and dislikes. Perhaps we found our identity in our friends or our
family. Maybe our identity, along with our security, was found in our
education, our job, or our athletic ability. Wherever we found it, when
we married we soon discovered that the things we found identity and
security in as a single person were not necessarily what would provide
identity and security within marriage. Marriage is a transition from
me to *us*, from independence to interdependence, and it takes growth

in our level of security to become a husband or a wife who can work at understanding and prioritizing the needs of another.

When we are not committed to this personal growth, we remain a *married single*; and the fact is, married singles do not stay married. They are unable to transition from single adult life to married adult life because they are unable to transition from me to us, from mine to ours. Insecurity keeps us separated. It will even keep our checking accounts separate. Why? There is a one-word answer to that question—*fear.*

Everyone feels insecure in one way or another. People can hide their insecurities in many ways. The mind is full of self-defense mechanisms that help us cover up our insecurities. For example, someone who is the "life of the party" may in reality be an introvert playing the extrovert to keep inner pain and insecurities from being discovered by others.

Insecurities are often the result of a traumatic event, something that caused great emotional upset, or even smaller, less significant traumas like repeated teasing, invalidation, or continual humiliation. This trauma may have been an accident or a violent act in which someone loved and depended on was injured, left the family, or died. Or it may have been a trauma in the form of physical, emotional, or sexual abuse. A significant tragedy, loss, or failure in life (e.g., divorce, bankruptcy, losing a job, failure in school, losing a friend, etc.) can also cause people to be insecure.

The way parents handle everyday conflicts between themselves as a couple and with others affects the emotional development of their children. When destructive marital conflict exists, children may lack confidence and become hesitant to move forward. Children raised in a chaotic, unpredictable, or volatile environment where they are kept off balance, on guard, or consistently on edge can develop insecurities. Because a child's emotional security is closely related to a happy marital life, parents must learn how to handle conflicts constructively for the sake of both their children and themselves.

A Picture of Insecurity

Growing up with an angry and physically abusive father, Greg (a real person in our lives) adopted mechanisms of self-protection. Those mechanisms kept him out of harm's way with his dad. He learned when to talk and when not to talk; he also learned that silence kept him from revealing his true self and his true emotions. Introversion protected an already fragile esteem and, in his environment, helped to prevent the experience of further pain.

Bringing those personal childhood precautions into marriage did not help Greg, however. His wife thought he became distant and quiet because of something she did or said. She continually second-guessed what he seemed to be thinking or feeling. Growing up, Greg's insecurities were a direct result of his fear of his father's abusive treatment. Today, even though he lives as an adult with a woman who loves him, he has been unsuccessful at overcoming this fear and being vulnerable with her. It is slowly killing his marriage. What once served a purpose and worked for him is now harmful and destructive. The inward silence speaks loudly to the very person he should feel most comfortable opening up to, his wife.

Other causes of insecurity can include:

- A poorly developed concept of oneself, brought on by a low or underdeveloped self-confidence

- Feelings of inadequacy

- A negative body image

- Never having felt accepted or approved of by others, especially those who were perceived as important in our life

- Unrealistic expectations by authority figures still trying to be met as an adult

Unfortunately, these long-term insecurities can become identities as well. For example:

- My drug or alcohol addiction becomes my identity.

- My sexual orientation is related to my identity.

- My religious upbringing is my identity.

- My family culture or ethnicity is my identity.

- Long-term sickness/preoccupation becomes my identity.

- My wealth is my hope and my identity.

- My education or my intellect is my identity.

- My abilities and talents, e.g., art, music or work gifts, are my identity.

THE IDOL OF SELF

When our identity becomes intertwined with our insecurity we can become steeped in self-adoration. Perhaps the most telling definition of long-term insecurity is that of the idol of self. It is to be preoccupied or consumed by your image, your own self-concern, your need of affirmation and attention from others (rather than from God). Exodus 34:13-14 tells us, "You must break down their pagan altars, smash their sacred pillars, and cut down their Asherah poles. You must worship no other gods, for the Lord, whose very name is Jealous, is a God who is jealous about his relationship with you" (NLT).

We bring these emotional insecurities and identities into our marriage, tending to look to our spouse to meet our unmet needs and provide all that we lacked in our lives prior to this relationship. This is unfair and unrealistic to our spouse.

Recently my (Steve's) mother handed me a lifetime of report cards. I couldn't believe she saved them after all those decades. I set the pile aside to perhaps discard them at a later date. In boredom one evening, I decided to pull them out and began to read. I had decent grades, but what really struck me were the teachers' comments. The one that still stands out to me was from kindergarten. It seems that I was too nervous to properly use scissors in cutting paper. Yep, I failed scissors cutting. So significant was this that the teacher actually noted it on my report card.

I was nervous because I was insecure. I didn't want to be there, I wanted to be at home with my mother. Home, in my backyard, was a safe place and this environment with twenty-some other kids was just plain chaotic and out of my control.

Insecurity can be overcome by understanding who God is and who we are in Him. (Note: See the "Who I Am In Christ" exercise at the end of this chapter.) We need to recognize that we will not find security in other people, in our job, or in circumstances (e.g., thinking that we will feel better about ourselves if we get a promotion, buy a nicer car, lose some weight). Security can only be found in the peace God offers through Jesus. It's important to embrace your identity as God's beloved child (see 1 John 3:2). We do not have to earn God's love; He loves us completely and unconditionally (see Jer. 31:3). His favor is based on His mercy, not on our desire or efforts (see Lam. 3:22-23).

We overcome insecurity when we refuse to dwell on our concerns and choose to pray about them instead, trusting God to guide us by His Holy Spirit. As we look to God—and not another person—to complete us, we overcome our unhealthy dependence on that person. God's strength and power help us to face whatever situations we encounter with confidence (see Rom. 8:37).

JESUS AND SECURITY

We love the illustration in the gospel of John personally given to us by Jesus one day when the Pharisees were confronting Him. These

Pharisees actually had the audacity to challenge Jesus over appearing as His own witness. You see, in the Old Testament every true witness was established by two or three corroborating testimonials. But Jesus' response was that His testimony was valid because, "I know where I came from and where I am going" (John 8:14). Jesus knew who He was, where He came from, why He was on the earth, and where He was going. Every human being is attempting to find the answers of why he or she is here, what he or she is called to do, and where he or she will spend eternity.

Just as Christ knew He was the "light of the world," we can know whose we are. There is no greater level of security than to know in our hearts that we are God's and He has a plan for our lives individually and, at the same time, together.

Finally, we overcome our insecurities by building healthy intimacy with God and others. Knowing the unconditional love of God brings healing to our deepest needs, causing us to experience freedom in our relationships with others, especially our spouse.

Questions to consider as individuals:

1. What insecurities do I deal with in my life?

2. Can I remember anything that happened in my past to cause my insecurities?

3. What are some of my beliefs that account for my insecurity?

4. What are some negative consequences I've experienced due to my insecurity?

5. How has my insecurity affected my marriage?

6. How can I change my ungodly beliefs about security into godly ones by the truth of God's Word?

7. Are there any ways I see in which my spouse helps to instill insecure feelings?

OUR CORE NEED

If we suffer from insecurity or feelings of low esteem and have identity issues prior to marriage, just saying the words "I do" will not change those issues in our lives.

The answer to low esteem is not high esteem. The answer is dying to ourselves: "For we know that our old self was crucified with him" (Rom. 6:6; see also Gal. 2:20). Even our Lord said that if we wanted to be His disciples, we must first deny ourselves and take up His cross and follow Him (see Matt. 16:24).

Do you think that Jesus had high or low esteem? We believe He had neither. Before Jesus did one miracle or preached His first message, before any of His public ministry began, He was baptized in the Jordan River by John. At that time, the Bible records the heavens opened and the Holy Spirit descended upon Jesus like a dove. Then the Father spoke from heaven something we find astounding: "You are my Son, whom I love; with you I am well pleased" (Mark 1:11).

God was *well pleased* and expressed His love for His Son before His Son accomplished anything miraculous on the earth. In order for Jesus to gain the Father's approval, all He had to do was be who He was—a son. God's approval did not come from Jesus' great works, great words, or great wisdom. His approval came by simply being who He was called to be without condition. Christ's esteem was found in His heavenly Father's approval.

This is precisely how the Father sees you. In fact, He says that before you were in your mother's womb, He knew you (see Jer. 1:5). God chose you from the foundations of the earth (see Eph. 1:4).

Esteem and identity come not from what you can do. They come from what Jesus has already done for you on the cross. You are His beloved son or daughter with whom He is well pleased. There is no justification (my efforts and attempts at self-approval) through anything we do. Only the Justifier, the Just One, can lead us to self-approval (see

Rom. 3-5). No matter how motivated, talented, or intelligent we are, we cannot gain security or significance (i.e., worth or value) through our own efforts. So, the conclusion is not the proverbial high esteem (whatever anyone subjectively feels that is), but rather something that we like to refer to as a *God-esteem*.

To truly grasp this concept requires a radical shift in thought. Simply trying to convince ourselves of who we are by repetitious thoughts cannot accomplish a changing of our patterns of thinking. This kind of change occurs only as the Holy Spirit brings revelation to our minds through our spirit, creating new thoughts. The process of change, then, is not from our mind to our spirit but from our spirit to our mind. Romans chapter 8 affirms this truth; these scriptures are life altering in the way they describe the process of change. Revealed is the fact that those who live according to their sinful nature have their minds set on what that nature desires. The sinful mind is filled with death, but the mind controlled by the Spirit is filled with life and full of peace. Those controlled by the Spirit please God, and we know that God lives in them.

Who is responsible for such significant change? We are individually responsible as we (re)train our spirit to listen to God's Spirit. For the Christian, change does not begin with a good idea or a goal, but by God's truth revealed to us in our spirit. That truth changes our beliefs, and when we believe correctly we will think correctly. If we think God's thoughts, we will complete His will, actually doing what God says we can do. It is a lifelong pursuit of hearing His voice and allowing Him to align our beliefs with His.

FURTHER STEPS TO HEALING INSECURITY

1. We must renounce the idol of worshiping oneself. There is only one God to worship, and it's not ourselves. We must take a stand to worship Him and Him alone. There must be no agreement between our self and idols (see 2 Cor. 6:16-18).

2. The Word of God is clear that God is our refuge, our High Tower, our Stronghold, and our Hiding Place. We cannot be that for ourselves (see Ps. 9:9; 31:4; 32:7).

3. Our security is fully and totally in His acceptance and approval (see Rom. 15:7).

4. The fear of man versus the fear of God—we must identify the difference (see Gal. 1:10). We must identity any spirit of fear and reject it (see Ps. 112:7-8).

5. We need to cut off the weights of perfectionism, constantly attempting to bring attention to ourselves and trying to live up to the expectations of others. Just before Paul's shipwreck he told the crew to cut off the anchors and leave them in the sea (see Acts 27:40). We must release the weights that hold us back and tie us down.

6. We must stop taking ourselves so seriously and be able to laugh at ourselves.

7. Find courage in the One who paid the price for our completeness, our security, and our wholeness. From the cross, Jesus breaks insecurity off of our life (see Gal. 3:13).

8. See the successes that already exist in our life. What healings have already taken place since we accepted Christ into our life? What healing still needs to take place to bring about security?

9. What are the misbeliefs that battle with our own security? What do we tell ourselves that agrees with insecurity versus what the Word of God says? See

Jeremiah 1:4-10—God's message was this: I knew you even before you were in the womb of your mother; I set you apart and I called/appointed you (see Eph. 1:4).

10. Know that God sees what others do or have done to us and that we do not need to defend ourselves or protect ourselves from hurt. The story related in Genesis 31:1-13 can be a helpful illustration. When Laban turned against Jacob, Jacob wisely noticed that Laban was not treating him as he once did. Jacob called his family together and said, "The God of my father has been with me. You know that I've worked for your father with all my strength, yet your father has cheated me by changing my wages ten times. ...So God has taken away your father's livestock and has given them to me" (Gen. 31:5-9). God saw all that Laban had done to Jacob, and Jacob would leave with more wealth than Laban.

Speak the following words of truth over yourself and one another as a prayer of spirit-to-mind renewal:

All the worth, all the value, all the esteem, all the security, all the significance, and all the identity I need is found in the One who already approves of me from the foundation of the earth, the One who knew me before I was found in my mother's womb. I am my Beloved's; He loves me; He is well pleased with me before I do or accomplish anything.

"Accept one another, then, *just as Christ accepted you,* in order to bring praise to God" (Rom. 15:7). This scripture literally says that the Son of God accepts you; therefore, accept one another. We cannot explain God's acceptance; we can only receive it for ourselves. Do not allow others to lie to you and continue to cause confusion and harm to your inner self. Realize and receive God's love and acceptance of you.

Why is a discussion about self-esteem, security, and insecurity so important in a book about marriage? If these issues are not settled and healed, we will look to our spouse to build our personal sense of worth and meet all of our needs for security. As we receive this revelation, our needs for worth and value through another, such as our spouse, can come to an end because those needs are already met through Christ.

Take a few minutes to dialogue together over the following questions:

1. How have we attempted to derive our worth from one another? What specific examples from our life together show this happening?

2. Prior to this revelation, how have we tried to earn approval and justification for ourselves from God? From one another?

3. To move from an unhealthy, self-centered me-esteem to a healthy God-esteem, we will need to have a...

Biblical Concept of Who I Am in Christ

Take the time to read and study the following verses. Through the prayerful study of these carefully selected scriptures, it is our belief these words can help to build a God-esteem. Record the scriptures that speak specifically to your area(s) of insecurity and meditate on the truth they reveal to you.

I am highly esteemed (Daniel 9:23).

I am now God's child (1 John 3:2).

I am born of the imperishable seed of God's Word (1 Peter 1:23).

I am loved by Christ and freed from my sins (Revelation 1:5).

I am forgiven all my sins (Ephesians 1:7).

I am justified from all things (Acts 13:39).

I am the righteousness of God (2 Corinthians 5:21).

I am free from all condemnation (Romans 8:1).

I am free from my past (Philippians 3:13).

I am a new creature (2 Corinthians 5:17).

I am the temple of the Holy Spirit (1 Corinthians 6:19).

I am redeemed from the curse of the law (Galatians 3:13).

I am reconciled to God (2 Corinthians 5:18).

I am loved; God's Son sacrificed Himself for me (1 John 4:10).

I am a saint and loved by God (Romans 1:7).

I am holy and without blame before Him (Ephesians 1:4).

I am the head and not the tail (Deuteronomy 28:13).

I am called of God by the grace given in Christ (2 Timothy 1:9).

I have been given fullness in Christ (Colossians 2:10).

I am rescued from the power of darkness (Colossians 1:13).

I am accepted by Christ (Romans 15:7).

I am the salt of the earth (Matthew 5:13).

I am the light of the world (Matthew 5:14).

I am dead to sin (Romans 6:2).

I am alive to God (Romans 6:11).

I am seated with Christ in heavenly realms (Ephesians 2:6).

I am a king and a priest to God (Revelation 1:6).

I am loved with an everlasting love (Jeremiah 31:3).

I am an heir of God, a joint heir with Christ (Romans 8:17).

I am qualified to share in the inheritance of the kingdom of light (Colossians 1:12).

I am more than a conqueror (Romans 8:37).

I am healed by the wounds of Jesus (1 Peter 2:24).

I was known by God before I was formed in the womb (Jeremiah 1:5; Ephesians 1:4).

I am in Christ Jesus by God's act (1 Corinthians 1:30).

I am kept by God's power (1 Peter 1:5).

I am sealed with the promised Holy Spirit (Ephesians 1:13).

I am not condemned; I have everlasting life (John 5:24).

I am crucified with Christ; nevertheless, I live (Galatians 2:20).

I have been given all things that pertain to life (2 Peter 1:3).

I have been blessed with every spiritual blessing (Ephesians 1:3).

I am a partaker of the divine nature (2 Peter 1:4).

I have peace with God (Romans 5:1).

I am a chosen royal priest (1 Peter 2:9).

I can do all things through Christ (Philippians 4:13).

I have all my needs met by God according to His riches in glory in Christ Jesus (Philippians 4:19).

I shall do even greater works than Christ Jesus (John 14:12).

I am kept strong and blameless to the end (1 Corinthians 1:8).

I am chosen by Him (1 Thessalonians 1:4).

I am born of God and I overcome the world (1 John 5:4).

I have a guaranteed inheritance (Ephesians 1:14).

I am a fellow citizen in God's household (Ephesians 2:19).

Christ's truth has set me free (John 8:32).

I always triumph in Christ (2 Corinthians 2:14).

I am in Jesus Christ's hands (John 10:28).

I am holy, without blemish and free from accusation (Colossians 1:22).

I have eyes to see God's eternal purpose (2 Corinthians 4:18).

Christ is being formed in me (Galatians 4:19).

I am anointed by the Holy One (1 John 2:20).

God's love is lavished upon me (1 John 3:1).

I am kept from falling and presented without fault (Jude 24).

I am God's house (Hebrews 3:6).

God has given me a spirit of power, of love, and of self-discipline (2 Timothy 1:7).

I am convinced that He is able to guard what I have entrusted to Him (2 Timothy 1:12).

He has considered me faithful and appointed me to His service (1 Timothy 1:12).

I am justified by faith (Romans 3:28).

The Spirit Himself intercedes for me (Romans 8:26).

Inwardly I am being renewed day by day (2 Corinthians 4:16).

For freedom Christ has set me free (Galatians 5:1).

I am held together by Him (Colossians 1:17).

I have the mind of Christ (1 Corinthians 2:16).

I am called to build Christ in others (Colossians 1:28).

According to the Word of God, we are spirit, soul, and body. Normally, we feed the body three meals a day. The soul is educated and fed emotionally. This exercise is designed to nourish the spirit—that part of us in which God dwells. Study these scriptures to discover who you are in Christ and provoke biblical change from the spirit to the mind and not the mind to the spirit (see Rom. 8:5-9). Read them over and over, allowing the truth of God's Word to set you free. You can even place your names within the context of the verse.

Chapter Three

THE "ONE" OF US

*To the world you might be one person, but
to one person you might be the world.*
—AUTHOR UNKNOWN

*When you realize you want to spend the rest
of your life with somebody, you want the rest
of your life to start as soon as possible.*
—AUTHOR UNKNOWN

Your marriage in and of itself is not the problem and never has been. Truthfully, it's the two individuals in the marriage who create the issues. The problem is *us*.

The fact is, men and women are not the same. This was a creative, intentional design by God, and the sooner we embrace this fact, the sooner we can move forward and grow as couples. We must make the decision to have our differences become our strengths and not our weaknesses. When two persons become one, parts of each must die. The newly married couple limps along trying to reconcile what they thought were similarities with what now seem much more like differences—often huge differences. Becoming one is a journey from the moment we say the words I do. And that journey will continue *as long as we both shall live.*

When we buy a new car, we enjoy the new-car smell. We appreciate the fact that it doesn't break down from age and worn parts. We love that it's clean and shiny, without a single stain on the carpet or scratch in the paint. However, unless we provide the proper maintenance in the months and years that follow, our car will eventually break down.

It's not necessarily bad or wrong for a marriage to run on "new" for a season. Because it's new, kindness abounds; disputes are short-lived; forgiveness comes easily. But when the new begins to fade, we tend to be less forgiving and extend less grace. Like the new car that begins to exhibit problems, has its dings and dents, and shows signs of wear, we become less concerned about its daily care and its future. In fact, we may even begin to dream about its replacement.

Thankfully, human relationships are different from cars. Old love is deeper and stronger than young love. As we age together, we can appreciate the differences rather than trying to make our spouse like us. The wise couple learns to use that "incompatibility"—those differences—to their advantage. They begin to learn that no team is made up of similar talent, and each member has a different strength to be used in a particular area. Just as in a healthy business, management acknowledges its own weaknesses and then hires those who can make up for those differences by bringing their strengths alongside a discerning leader. As our marriage matures, we learn to not be threatened by those strengths. We begin to realize that God called together this team of two to become one.

Speaking of differences, when we were first married we quickly discovered that we had differing financial values. I (Steve) thought that Mary was a "loose spender." And Mary thought that I was a "tight saver." If we had any major difference in those years, it was about money. However, once we began to discover the strengths in our differences, we became a dynamic financial team. Mary loved to give, to sow financial seed, and to share with those in need. I needed to learn to value and adapt to her freedom to give. After all, you will reap what you sow, right? Mary, on the other hand, needed what I had to offer in growing a savings account and having an emergency fund so that we could stay out of debt. When we drew on one another's financial strengths, it became a win-win area of our marriage, a positive out of a potential negative. We will discuss these differences and how we relate through them later in the book.

Complete the following statements with what first comes to mind. Do these exercises separately.

ASSESS US (WIFE)

1. The word that best describes our marriage is

_____

2. The strongest area of our marriage is

_____

_____

_____

3. The weakest area of our marriage is

_____

_____

_____

4. I tend to hurt my spouse when

_____

_____

_____

5. My spouse tends to hurt me when

_____

_____

_____

6. My love language is

_____

_____

_____

7. My spouse's love language is

_____

_____

_____

8. My spouse laughs when I

_____

_____

_____

9. I laugh when my spouse

_____

_____

_____

10. I feel inadequate around my spouse when

_____

_____

_____

11. I feel honored when my spouse

_____

_____

_____

12. My spouse feels honored when I

_____

_____

_____

13. I feel unity in our marriage when

_____

_____

_____

14. I feel disunity in our marriage when

_____

_____

_____

15. I know my spouse is angry when

_____

_____

_____

16. My spouse knows I am angry when

_____

_____

_____

17. An area of security in our marriage is

_____

_____

_____

18. An area of insecurity in our marriage is

_____

_____

_____

19. I feel valued by my spouse when

_____

_____

_____

20. My spouse feels valued by me when

_____

_____

_____

21. I admire my spouse when

_____

_____

_____

22. My spouse admires me when

_____

_____

_____

23. My spouse seeks my opinion when

_____

_____

_____

24. I seek my spouse's opinion when

_____

_____

_____

25. I am proud of my spouse when

_____

_____

_____

26. My spouse is proud of me when

_____

_____

_____

27. I feel my spouse is selfish when

_____

_____

_____

28. My spouse feels I am selfish when

_____

_____

_____

29. I trust my spouse to

_____

_____

_____

30. My spouse trusts me to

_____

_____

_____

ASSESS US (HUSBAND)

1. The word that best describes our marriage is

_____

2. The strongest area of our marriage is

_____

_____

_____

3. The weakest area of our marriage is

_____

_____

_____

4. I tend to hurt my spouse when

_____

_____

_____

5. My spouse tends to hurt me when

_____

_____

_____

6. My love language is

_____

_____

_____

7. My spouse's love language is

_____

_____

_____

8. My spouse laughs when I

_____

_____

_____

9. I laugh when my spouse

_____

_____

_____

10. I feel inadequate around my spouse when

_____

_____

_____

11. I feel honored when my spouse

_____

_____

_____

12. My spouse feels honored when I

_____

_____

_____

13. I feel unity in our marriage when

_____

_____

_____

14. I feel disunity in our marriage when

_____

_____

_____

15. I know my spouse is angry when

_____

_____

_____

16. My spouse knows I am angry when

_____

_____

_____

17. An area of security in our marriage is

_____

_____

_____

18. An area of insecurity in our marriage is

_____

_____

_____

19. I feel valued by my spouse when

_____

_____

_____

20. My spouse feels valued by me when

_____

21. I admire my spouse when

22. My spouse admires me when

23. My spouse seeks my opinion when

24. I seek my spouse's opinion when

25. I am proud of my spouse when

26. My spouse is proud of me when

27. I feel my spouse is selfish when

_____

_____

_____

28. My spouse feels I am selfish when

_____

_____

_____

29. I trust my spouse to

_____

_____

_____

30. My spouse trusts me to

_____

_____

_____

OUR MARRIAGE STORY

What is your marriage story? If you plan on having children some-day, what will you tell them when they ask how you met and how you fell in love? The things that brought you together as a couple can often be the things that help keep you together. The following questions will help you remember your marriage story. Take some time to ask each other for an honest response to the following questions.

1. What were the qualities that attracted you to me?

2. What made our courtship worth pursuing?

3. What differences did we encounter during engagement?

4. How did we deal with those differences at the time?

5. Create a list of the ten best traits that we admired about one another when we said, "I do."*

6. What did we enjoy most about our first year of marriage?

7. What were the more challenging areas during our first year of marriage?

8. We're still married today because…

9. How has our commitment to this marriage union changed over the course of time?

10. Having considered our story, what positive ingredient from the past is missing in the present?

*Returning to question number five, we recommend keeping this list (of at least ten items) in your wallet or purse or some frequently visible place and pulling it out every once in a while to remind yourself of the things that you absolutely love about and attracted you to your spouse.

WHAT IS THE PURPOSE OF THIS THING WE CALL MARRIAGE?

In your own words, define marriage:

_____

_____

_____

_____

_____

_____

What, in your opinion, is the purpose of marriage?

_____

_____

_____

_____

_____

There are many well-known passages in the Bible that discuss the topic of marriage. Proverbs 18:22 reveals that if you find a wife, you find a "good thing." Proverbs 31 describes how precious a woman of God is, and Ephesians 5 goes into detail about the marriage relationship. It describes marriage as a picture of Christ and His church, how He loves and cares for His church as a man does his wife. The Bible also says that marriage is a mystery and that from it, we replenish the earth.

But we want to take you to two different, and perhaps unlikely, scriptures that we feel describe the very purpose of this gift we call marriage:

*We proclaim him, admonishing and teaching everyone with all wisdom, so that **we may present everyone perfect in Christ** (Colossians 1:28).*

*My dear children, for whom I am again in the pains of childbirth until **Christ is formed in you** (Galatians 4:19).*

Paul was a spiritual father, a disciple called to disciple others. His goal was to build Christ in his sons and daughters in the faith. Similarly, our goal as husbands and wives should be to build Christ in one other. *Building Christ* then becomes the purpose of marriage. Let us explain.

To build is to encourage, to support, to speak into, to love, to care for—all actions that, if brought into the marriage relationship, provide the necessary ingredients for oneness. When you make "the life of Christ" the desired outcome of this building, you incorporate the spiritual dimension of the incarnate One, God in us as human beings. As the Father, the Son, and the Holy Spirit are One and would never do or say anything that would be contradictory to who They are, so God has called husband and wife to be one. And in Christ's oneness with His Father, we know that the many traits of Christ include, but certainly are not limited to: unconditional and sacrificial love; a servant's heart; One who does not desire His own will but the will of the Father, who ultimately laid down His life for us.

Practically, to build the life of Christ means that everything I think, say, and do must be filtered through this question: *Is what I am thinking, is what I am about to say or do going to build Christ in my spouse?* This type of transformational thinking could alter every marriage on earth. To speak and to act like Christ toward one another may seem simple and basic, but it is not easy. If you memorize the question above and consider it when interacting with your spouse, it will change your marriage. And, with the Holy Spirit's help, it will change you, too.

This principle of the purpose of marriage—building Christ—is a radical change for some. I (Steve) found myself one day sitting in my office across from a couple who were pouring out their hearts to me. As the husband described the domestic violence with which he grew up, he was at the same time confessing to physical abuse within his own marriage.

While his wife was in tears and he was feeling so much shame, I began to share how this "generational sin" was handed down to him (see 1 Pet. 1:18). I continued with Exodus 20:5, which states that the iniquity of the fathers extends to the third and fourth generation, but through the cross he could walk in freedom and that Galatians 3:13 reveals Jesus became a curse for us, that He is the ultimate curse-breaker. The cross of Jesus breaks the sins of the fathers, preventing those sins from becoming an inheritance for their sons.

A generational sin is like a generational disease. Medical science teaches us that certain medical conditions are genetic or have the possibility of being inherited. Like the physical realm of life, the soul realm has a way of traveling through family lines. Examples of this concept might be domestic violence, certain fears, or phobias.

Together, we prayed a prayer of deliverance from this sin, along with confession and repentance. With deep sorrow and regret, he asked his wife to forgive him. He prayed and released his father from the sin committed against him and his family. It was a powerful step of faith that brought tremendous freedom to him as he forgave his father.[1]

It was then that I shared this principle of building Christ in his wife. I went directly to that phrase, "If what I am thinking or what I am about to say or do is not going to build Christ, then it must change." With the scriptural mandate, a specific prayer, and committing this important thought to memory, the husband felt like he had a practical tool to change his life and the life of his marriage.

While Philippians 2 may not mention marriage specifically, it unquestionably provides a scriptural overview of what we are attempting to communicate to you:

> *If you have any encouragement from being united with Christ, if any comfort from his love, if any fellowship with the Spirit, if any tenderness and compassion, then make my joy complete by being like-minded, having the same love, being one in spirit and purpose. Do nothing out of selfish ambition or vain conceit, but in humility consider others* [your spouse] *better than yourselves. Each of you should look not only to your own interests, but also to the interests of others* [your spouse] (Philippians 2:1-4).

Discuss the following questions:

1. How can we grow spiritually and emotionally so that we move away from selfishness and move toward selflessness?

2. What are the areas we can identify that may not be "building the life of Christ" in my mate?

3. What are some practical ways in which we can build the life of Christ in one another?

4. Do we know another couple whose marriage exemplifies this lifestyle who would be willing to mentor us in this definition of the purpose of marriage?

ASSESSING OUR EXPECTATIONS

As we discover more and more how to build Christ in another, we can also begin to more easily identify our expectations. Some expectations are spoken and some are left unspoken. In other words, we have them, but we fail to communicate them. Unmet expectations are often the root cause of disappointment, and ongoing unmet expectations can be damaging to our relationship. Further, ongoing unmet expectations are not something we tend to embrace, but with much patience can handle for short seasons. However, when unmet expectations become the norm, we will look for other ways to fill the void or in anger become demanding of our spouse. Take some time to discuss your responses to the following questions concerning expectations.

1. What are your top five expectations (met or unmet) of your spouse?

2. When an expectation is met, what is your response to your spouse?

3. When an expectation is not met, what is your response to your spouse?

4. Do you have any expectations that, according to your spouse, are unreasonable? If so, discuss them.

5. How can you make unreasonable expectations more reasonable?

When expectations are continually not met, they can become demands on our part. Have you felt demands from your spouse and have you placed demands upon your spouse? How can we effectively release one another from our demands so that we can better concentrate on building Christ in each other?

Perhaps this will sound radical, but suppose we fully release our expectations of our spouse? Then, when an expectation is met it will be an added blessing. The reward of being released and of releasing our expectations will far outweigh any loss. In the end, when the pressure is off, the inner desire will be to move toward meeting expectations.

LEAVING AND CLEAVING TOWARD MARRIAGE ONENESS

The following scriptural study gives you the opportunity to discover what we feel could be God's primary values and expectations for marriage. Review the scriptures together with each other, your marriage mentors, or small group.

Genesis 1:25-27

This is the place to start. God had a specific design in mind when He created humankind and instituted marriage. We were designed in His image, His likeness. He gave us dominion over the animals of the earth. God created us both male and female.

Genesis 2:7, 21-22

Man was made from the dust of the earth, and God breathed the breath of life into him. Woman was created from man. She was specifically designed to correspond to the man. Eve was "fashioned," while Adam was "formed."

Genesis 2:18

Man's first need from God was a "helper suitable for him." God solved the first problem that man encountered—loneliness. As Adam named the animals, he noticed that none of them was even close to being "suitable" or one of his kind.

Genesis 2:23; Ephesians 5:31

Eve was given to Adam by God, and Adam said, "This is now bone of my bones and flesh of my flesh; she shall be called 'woman,' for she was taken out of man." Eve was physically, spiritually, intellectually, emotionally, and relationally suitable for Adam. She was not like the animals. She was of the same flesh. A part of Adam's structure was used to fashion Eve. From the beginning, God has had an established order, and in His creative wisdom He called one man to one woman.

Genesis 2:24; Matthew 19:4-5; Mark 10:6-8

Before joining and cleaving, there first needs to be a leaving. We leave our parents to establish a new family unit without cohabitation first. The focus becomes one another. Former friends, jobs, and extended family take on a lesser priority than this new union. This new household is under new authority. One man (the father) walks the bride up the wedding aisle; then another man (the new husband) walks her back down the aisle.

Genesis 2:25; Ephesians 5:31-32

Marriage means that two persons become one. Kevin is Sarah, and Sarah is Kevin. What affects Sarah affects Kevin. These two persons are now united. This union was designed to be heterosexual and monogamous (see Prov. 5:15-23; 6:23-33). There are three expressions of oneness in Scripture:

- The Trinity (2 Cor. 13:14)
- Christ and the Church (Eph. 5:25-27; 31-32)
- Marriage (Gen. 2:24; Eph. 5:31)

One cannot be divided without the result being two halves. Separation or divorce is a separation of one person. This separation, it is said, leaves two fractions of one whole.

Prior to Genesis 3, we see Adam and Eve partnering together with God for marriage oneness. With the fall of mankind in Genesis 3 comes the brokenness of marriage oneness within God's original design. However, Christ became the second Adam for the healing of this brokenness (see 1 Cor. 15:22, 45-49). Every marriage longs for the partnering described in Genesis 1 and 2, working together as a single unit for the common good of the marriage and family.

This "partnering" is the provision our Father has redeemed for us through the cross of His Son. This oneness found in the Trinity and in Christ and His Church is the oneness we too can find in our partnering together. In pursuit of this partnering, we are returning to the garden of God's presence in our marriage on a daily basis. Marriages that partner together sincerely represent the image and likeness of God from the Garden of Eden before the fall of man.

Take some time to discuss the following:

1. How have you been specifically designed to correspond with one another through your male and female differences?

2. Adam needed Eve as Eve needed Adam. How do you "need" one another?

3. Marriage means that two persons become one. What affects you affects your spouse. Share some examples of this concept from your marriage.

4. How are we called to partner together in our oneness?

MARRIAGE ONENESS

As followers of Christ who are filled with the Holy Spirit, it becomes our desire to be in unity with the Spirit. While we maintain our unique personalities, our goal is to become one with the very Spirit of God so that in our heart we know, understand, and act upon the will of the Father, "That all of them may be one, Father, just as you are in me and I am in you. May they also be in us so that the world may believe that you have sent me" (John 17:21). This is not the Holy Spirit coming upon us or taking over our spirit for a specific one-time task, but instead uniting with our spirit in order to accomplish the goal of oneness with the triune God.

Marriage is much like this. At your wedding ceremony, you began the becoming-one process. While you are still two distinct personalities, you ideally act in the best interests of the other. This is similar to the fact that while we are still human, we act toward the interests of the Father and His direction for our lives. In order to become one, we focus our hearts and minds on our spouse, and then our thoughts are filled with how to please and serve him or her. We become one in our souls and in our goals and desires for a long-lasting marriage that honors God and one another. Becoming one is a purposeful act, and if we please the Father we are sure to please our soul mate.

SPEAKING ONENESS

Oneness begins with our spoken vows before God.

> *If a man makes a vow to the Lord, or swears an oath to bind himself by some agreement, he shall not break his word; he shall do according to all that proceeds out of his mouth* (Numbers 30:2 NKJV).

Few of us really understood what it meant to speak our marriage vows to one another before both God and witnesses. Few of us realized the depth of commitment that it would take to walk out those vows in actual life circumstances.

Webster defines a vow as *a solemn promise or pledge that commits one to act or behave in a particular way.* But marriage vows are more than just a promise or a pledge. According to Scripture, marriage is a covenant to companionship, and a covenant was the most binding agreement in existence. It was an oath that came with great penalties if broken.

Your vows are spoken to one another before God and those who witness your marriage ceremony. God takes this covenant quite seriously, and so should we. Listen to what the book of Ecclesiastes states concerning a vow: "When you make a vow to God, do not delay to pay it; for He has no pleasure in fools. Pay what you have vowed—better not to vow than to vow and not pay" (Eccles. 5:4-5 NKJV).

There should be no consideration given to the breaking of a marriage vow. When vows are broken, particularly wedding vows, God's heart is broken even more than ours. Jesus urged, "What God has joined together, let man not separate" (Mark 10:9).

For the following exercise, you will need to locate your marriage vows. They may be in your wedding album or can be found on your wedding video. Retrieve and review them, then discuss the following questions:

1. As we review those vows spoken years ago, what are our first thoughts?

2. What steps have we taken throughout our marriage to keep and honor those words we spoke to one another?

3. Would we change anything if we were to rewrite our vows today?

4. What steps can we take to help create a continuum of honoring our vows?

Now take a moment to reaffirm those vows that you made with each other and perhaps spend a moment in prayer thanking God for your life together.

The one of us—we are a powerful union who has the opportunity to grow closer each and every day of maintaining unreserved commitment to our vows.

NOTE

1. What is the root cause of domestic violence? It's an important question and one for which there is an answer from God's Word. We believe the divinely inspired words found in Ephesians 5 provide the answer. In this chapter, husbands are commanded to love their wives and wives are to be submissive to their

husbands. Verse 26 tells husbands to love their wives as Jesus loved the church. Verses 26 and 27 states that Jesus, through His love, cleanses His bride and will present her to Himself without blemish. Then in verses 28 and 29 we are told, "In this same way, husbands ought to love their wives as their own bodies. He who loves his wife loves himself. After all, no one ever hated his own body, but he feeds and cares for it, just as Christ does the church." Where does domestic violence come from according to these scriptural insights? Self-hate. Out of our own self-hate, we hate or abuse others.

Chapter Four

HEALTHY BOUNDARIES FOR A HEALTHY RELATIONSHIP

*I love being married. It's so great to find that one special
person you want to annoy for the rest of your life.*
—RITA RUDNER

*He felt now that he was not simply close to her, but
that he did not know where he ended and she began.*
—LEO TOLSTOY, *Anna Karenina*

Healthy relationships bring happiness to our lives. They add
fun, reduce stress, and decrease anxiety as we give love to
and receive love from the people around us. The opposite is true
of unhealthy relationships. They increase stress and anxiety in our
lives. They bring broken hearts and spirits. Unhealthy relationships
did not start in the 1930s during the Great Depression, in the '60s
or the '70s with the sexual revolution, or even in this century. They
started in Genesis 3, when man walked away from an intimate relationship with his Creator and experienced a broken relationship
with the One closest to him.

CURSE-FILLED RELATIONSHIPS
VERSUS HEALTHY BOUNDARIES

"In a curse-filled marriage, one partner makes demands on the other as if he/she were the source rather than the resource."[1]

In Genesis 3, Adam and Eve disobeyed God by crossing the boundary God set for them and suffered the consequences of a broken relationship with God and one another. Their sons, Cain and Abel, the very next generation, experienced such brokenness in their curse-filled relationship that Cain murdered his brother.

For relationships to be healthy, they must have boundaries. What does this mean? Literally, boundaries are the physical, emotional, sexual, and spiritual limits we place on a relationship. Unhealthy relationships do not respect these limits; they cross boundaries all the time (for example, abuse of any kind, from manipulation, demands, unrealistic expectations, or loss of freedom to even more severe abuses). Dysfunctional families continually cross these lines. Often parents manipulate their children and children their parents.

In contrast to healthy relationships, unhealthy relationships can be codependent or emotionally dependent. Codependency means being directly connected to others' wrong or dysfunctional behavior by attempting to rescue, control, or fix them to make them happy. Emotional dependency reinforces the idea that another person can provide for all of your needs of security and nurture, making you emotionally dependent upon him or her. That is because, "Most dependent relationships are ingrown. Healthy relationships are open to others."[2]

If we don't maintain an awareness of our distinction from others (where one person ends and the other begins), we will be incapable of being who God has called us to be as a healthy individual. Instead, we will attempt to be who we think another desires us to become. If we do not set healthy boundaries for ourselves, we empower others to manipulate and control us to be who they need us to be (to meet their own personal needs) rather than who God has designed us to be. Oneness within a marriage relationship is never about control or manipulation but, rather, love that respects personal boundaries.

I (Mary) love a good chick flick, and the movie *Runaway Bride* is one of my favorites. The bride (played by Julia Roberts) could never go through with her multiple weddings because she was constantly attempting to be who she thought her groom desired her to be. She was unable to be herself; consequently, fear would set in as she approached the altar. Following the fear, she would go into flight mode, abandoning her fiancés.

In homes where alcoholism and drug addiction exist, codependency is often an issue for the family. Abusive parents who continually violate boundaries tend to raise damaged and broken, often emotionally dependent children looking for safety and security. When individual identity is lost in these types of dysfunctional families, family members begin to draw their sense of worth from others. Unfortunately, those "others" can be damaged persons themselves, and this can create a love/hate relationship or a co- or emotionally dependent relationship. In both of these situations, one person is looking to another for esteem, identity, security, and significance rather than to God (see Gal. 1:10; 1 Thess. 2:4-6).

Kevin and Michelle were a couple we had the opportunity to meet with on a regular basis for pre- and post-marital counseling. Kevin grew up in a family that constantly crossed boundaries, and this planted the seed for unhealthy relationships in his life. When Kevin married Michelle, he lacked a sense of security, a healthy identity, and a healthy esteem. Michelle realized early on that Kevin was dependent upon her for these emotional necessities. Trying to be his wife, parent, counselor, friend, and never-ending source of approval quickly depleted her. His appetite for these important areas of life was insatiable, and it was eroding their young love.

Because dysfunctional families create an environment of false guilt, family members can feel manipulated into taking responsibility for other family members' well-being or failures. This is what Kevin dealt with growing up, and what Michelle was now forced to face.

Healthy relationships, on the other hand, grow out of our ability to take ownership for our unhealthy family of origin or prior relationships and our ability to break those ongoing curse-filled relationships. Healthy relationships come by showing forgiveness and humility toward those who modeled unhealthy relationships to us. If Jesus had a prescription pad, it would read, "Forgive as you have been forgiven."

Healthy relationships are also a result of growth and maturity. An immature person sees a relationship as a means to an end (having his or her needs met first). This is why teenagers go in and out of relationships so quickly. If this immature practice hasn't stopped upon entering adulthood, it can lead to a pattern of selfish, curse-filled relationships.

ASSESSING THE HEALTH OF OUR FAMILY OF ORIGIN'S BOUNDARIES

1. Share some of the healthy boundaries your family of origin maintained.

2. Share some of the unhealthy boundaries you can identify.

3. How can we in our marriage move away from the unhealthy boundaries we have each identified?

Whenever we have the opportunity to speak to singles, one of the things we feel is most important to emphasize is to encourage them not to pursue marriage but rather to pursue maturity. When two immature individuals come together, their ultimate goal is to have their needs met solely by the other. When they come to the realization that this expectation is not going to be met, they often move on to the next relationship, hoping that it will be "the one." Invariably, "the one" never comes because these individuals are not maturing enough to grow out of their own selfishness.

Mature individuals, however, are healthy enough out of their own personal wholeness not to demand or continually take from their spouse or significant other; they can give freely of themselves. Healthy and mature singles give out of a personal sense of security and a healthy sense of esteem. In other words, they are able to love as they desire to be loved.

Healthy relationships flow out of a healthy relationship with God (see John 17:6-26; Eph. 5:25-29). In John 17, Jesus is conversing with His Father, saying, "I am yours; you gave me these disciples, and now they are yours again" (author's paraphrase). Jesus was not asking for an extension on the earth or asking the Father to allow His disciples to ascend with Him. While He had lived with them, trained them, and ministered to them for the last three and a half years, He never lost sight of who He was and who they were. He maintained healthy relationships with appropriate boundaries, even though they were intimate in their ministry together.

John 4:13-26 tells the story of the woman at the well. Jesus has a very personal encounter with this woman, a very needy woman—one who had five husbands and was now living with another man who was not her husband. His message to her was very clear—men would not meet her needs. He was the Living Water for whom she was so desperately searching. She had crossed appropriate boundaries, and the Savior was calling her to Himself—a safe, pure relationship that would quench her thirst for a lifetime.

1. How can unhealthy (curse-filled) boundaries in our marriage or family help to create unhealthy relationships?

2. Share some ways in which your relationship has continued to become a healthier relationship over your years of marriage.

3. What are some boundaries that you now have in place that help to create healthy relationship?

4. Can you identify a few areas where you can move toward maturity and become even more emotionally and spiritually healthy with God and with one another?

BOUNDARY PERCEPTIONS OF MY SPOUSE

Below you are given the opportunity to assess the boundaries of your spouse. Use different colored pens (his and hers) to mark your answers. Be honest, and remember that these are just your perceptions.

	NEEDS TO IMPROVE	IMPROVING	GOOD	VERY GOOD
INDIVIDUAL IDENTITIES				
TRUST				
FINANCES				
JEALOUSY				
MUTUAL RESPECT				
AFFIRMATION				
TEMPER				
DEPENDABILITY				

	NEEDS TO IMPROVE	IMPROVING	GOOD	VERY GOOD
JOB (RESPONSIBILITY/ TIME GIVEN)				
RECREATION (TIME BALANCE)				
TELEVISION (TIME BALANCE)				
TELEPHONE/ COMPUTER USE				
SECURITY				
FRIENDSHIPS				
PRAYING TOGETHER				
SPENDING TIME WITH YOU				
RELATIVES (RELATIONSHIPS/ INTERACTION)				
HONESTY				
TIME WITH GOD				
COMMUNICATION				

Be sure to affirm one another in the categories that you are each doing well in. Then take some time to look back over this exercise and consider the "Needs to Improve" areas. Talk about how we desire to improve. Discuss options for change that will give room for the necessary time and grace to make important changes.

TWELVE VALUES FOUND IN HEALTHY MARRIAGE RELATIONSHIPS

Let's move on to consider 12 healthy values that Mary and I ascribe to that maintain healthy boundaries within a marriage relationship. These values may not all be expressed maturely in any given relationship but are expressed with ease in most transparent relationships.

1. Love

Love is central to a healthy relationship because it does not seek its own health and blessing; rather, it pursues the health and blessing of the other. Love protects rather than exposes. Love believes in the relationship and that love holds all other areas together. Love allows and encourages differing emotional responses (see 1 Cor. 13). When love is not present, mistrust, fear, selfishness, and self-protection will develop.

2. Trust

Healthy relationships are built on trust, and trust takes time. If trust is growing, then fear, manipulation, and jealousy are not part of the relationship. Trust means we can release our partners to be who they are and do what they are called to do. We can share deeply, without fear of retribution. When trust is missing or waning, the marriage relationship can become cold, stagnant, and grow in antagonistic attitudes toward one other.

3. Mutual Respect and Honor

Each person cares about the other and allows personal decisions and choices. Mutual respect does not force someone to do something he or she is not comfortable doing. In this mutual respect, expectations remain realistic, and it is neither person's goal to change the other. Honor travels with respect because we will not honor someone we do not respect. To honor is to give our time to something or someone whom we determine to be more important than ourselves. Same-sex friendships often provide an environment of safety through mutual respect, and so it should be within marriage. When we feel unable to freely offer respect and follow through with honor toward our life mate, our relationship can become caustic and even abusive.

4. Boundaries

I can be me, you can be you, and we respect each other's limits. We do not attempt to manipulate those limits in order to gain something for ourselves from others; neither do we allow others to manipulate us. We make room for one another's personal preferences. Boundaries not maintained create a situation of marriage partners not knowing the limits of the relationship. We will not know or be able to identify where we each begin and end. The lack of boundaries causes confusion with roles, loyalties, and marital needs.

5. Affirmation

We can affirm one another and not compete with one another. We desire the best for the other and are pleased at his or her success. Both parties feel valued for who they are and do not feel as though they must work to earn this value. Healthy relationships affirm you to be you and lack critical judgment. (Another person who you value can place a judgment upon you, like a parent. This judgment does not allow for you to be you, criticizes your person, and offers no allowance for change.) Unhealthy relationships lack the freedom to express yourself without feeling as though you must brace yourself for the storm that will inevitably follow.

6. Security

Healthy persons do not allow their relationships to define them and do not compare themselves to or compete with others. They are secure in who they are and do not feel the need to perform. Similarly, healthy relationships do not invite comparison or competition that will make one person feel inadequate and the other superior. Rather, they foster a mutually edifying relationship wherein both persons feel confident (see 2 Cor. 10:12; 1 Cor. 3:1-9).

7. *Communication*

Healthy relationships involve lots of communication. Both persons not only talk but listen and respect what the other person is saying, even if they disagree (see Prov. 18:13). Conversation is always valued. Responses are appropriate and are not reactive or combative in nature (see Eph. 4:31-32). There is never a "seen and not heard" component. Praying together is another means of communication that is key to a healthy relationship. Engaging in the silent treatment never fixes anything; rather, it creates a higher level of volatile frustration.

8. *Shared Faith*

Faith is shared and not lorded over or manipulated into one party's belief. Faith is supportive to the relationship. Shared faith brings the power of spiritual alignment and agreement (see Amos 3:3; Deut. 6:4-9). When a couple does not share faith, they are missing the major component of connecting in the spiritual realm. The loss of that connection creates a deficit in us as human beings, created in the image of God.

9. *Disagreement without Disunity*

Fair fighting is a part of a healthy relationship, with the goal of achieving growth from differences and coming to a win-win resolution whenever possible. Equality is honored and helps maintain balance in the relationship. One person is not always right, and compromise is a main ingredient to solving conflict (see James 3:13-4:2). Conflict left unresolved builds disunity.

10 *Forgiveness*

Both persons walk in humility and are able to forgive and be forgiven without fear of shame. This causes the relationship to grow through hurt and pain rather than become arrested by it. An unforgiving heart will hinder emotional growth (see Col. 3:13; Heb. 12:14-15). When forgiveness is not given or received without condition, a root of bitterness can grow between you.

11. Honesty

Healthy relationships are full of truth, which allows the relationship to grow in trust and respect. Functional relationships are not built on a foundation of lies or deception but rather on a foundation of truth, even when the truth feels initially hurtful. The truth is always spoken in love and is full of grace (see Eph. 4:15). When truth is not spoken in love and grace, it can be used as a weapon to hurt the one who hurt us. The often spoken phrase, "The truth hurts" is not one we ever recommend you use because what it can actually mean is, "My truth is *the* truth; too bad that it hurts."

12. Individual Identities

Individual identities remain intact in healthy relationships. There is no enmeshment, but both parties enjoy a healthy interdependence. There is a mutual give and take that prevents domination by one personality. An individual identity means that we are able to receive the love of God and therefore can love our spouse through healthy self-love. We do not lose our identity by attempting to be another person's identity for him or her (see 1 John 3:1-3). When we lose our individual identities, we can begin to form an unhealthy emotional attachment.

With the above characteristics, we create an environment for personal growth and maturity. Relationships that are unhealthy, however, will inhibit both personal and marital growth. In the chapters that follow, we will discuss some of these values more deeply.

Consider the following questions together:

1.   Looking back over the 12 values of a healthy relationship, which are we most successful with?

2. Which values can we affirm our spouse in?

3. Has either of us been involved in a relationship that inhibited personal growth? Can we identify any brokenness from our past that affects our present relationship (i.e., trust issues, broken boundaries, unhealthy performance, or competition)?

4. Can we take a step of faith, confess our faults to one another, and pray for one another (see James 5:16)?

5. How can we embrace where we are in our relationship while simultaneously expressing faith for change in the future through affirmation, forgiveness, and agreement?

6. What values would you each add to the above list? In other words, beyond the mentioned 12, what other values are nonnegotiable for your marriage relationship?

Throughout this chapter, we have taken an in-depth look at the two of you as a couple. We the authors realize that it is challenging to be completely honest, but as you continue in this process you will see that change is possible. We desire that you go beyond challenge and pursue individual change. When two individuals are committed to personal change, we guarantee that you will see key improvements within your marriage.

NOTES

1. Jeffrey VanVonderen, *Families Where Grace Is in Place* (Minneapolis, MN: Bethany House Publishers, 1992), 25.
2. Steve Prokopchak, *Recognizing Emotional Dependency* (House to House Publications, 2003).

Chapter Five

MOVING BEYOND OUR HISTORIES

Take away love and our earth is a tomb.
—ROBERT BROWNING

Who being loved is poor?
—OSCAR WILDE

After participating in premarital counseling with literally dozens of couples, one common thread of belief that most of these couples seem to have is their self-perceived ability to communicate openly, lovingly, and deeply with one another. Meeting with many of those same couples for post-marital counseling, communication seems to be the common issue with which they all struggle. How can we feel so good about communication prior to marriage and feel the opposite about it after?

Prior to marriage, we spend hours communicating face to face and, when apart, by phone, text message, e-mail, and Facebook. We study one another and practice our listening skills to really hear each other's hearts. We attempt to win the other through our attentiveness, our affirmation, our words of love, and our body language of acceptance. One couple told us communication was so easy and came so naturally to them that they could not understand what the big deal was about the subject of communication within marriage.

Nothing magical happens when we say, "I do." There are no internal switches that turn on or off to inhibit the flow of communication. However, in many ways the pursuit is over. The other-focus can begin to return to self-focus and our own particular needs now that our partner has officially and publicly committed to being ours, "until death do us part." The areas that you had the patience to overlook prior to marriage often become stumbling blocks in the first year of marriage. That which you once shrugged off as cute is now irritating.

What happened? Were we faking it? Were we trying to expose only our good side? It was fun having our heads in the clouds and not needing to worry about all that could go wrong. Reality during engagement is different from reality during marriage, neither of which is necessarily good or bad. So, what's the issue?

INDEPENDENCE

We were created by God to live in a Genesis 1 and 2 world, but we find ourselves living in a Genesis 3 world. In the book of beginnings, there was clear and open communication between God and humanity. In fact, God would come to Adam in the garden and talk with him (Gen. 3:8-9). But after sin came and separated us from our Creator, communication became challenging in a world of fallen natures. God created us for relationship with Him and others, but at times we personally long for independence from both.

We will never forget when our son, who was 14 years old at the time, told us that he couldn't wait to leave our home. He wanted to watch a TV show that we said was off-limits. This is a common occurrence with teenagers—they long for independence but simply do not have the authority or the means to act upon that independence. Teenagers inwardly desire authority but cannot take full responsibility. As human beings, we seem to long for independence, but the truth is that nowhere in life can we act independently of others. Adam and Eve longed for their independence because the evil one told them they could be like God. But what they received was separation from God, the One who created them to be able to relate in a healthy manner, a manner that was not longing for independence and was not full of selfish desire.

Isaiah 14:12-15 provides insight into this independence syndrome. These scriptures open a window to see the inner desire of Lucifer in his personal competition with God. His outward expression recorded in this portion of Scripture tells us what was in his heart; five times he said the words *I will*—"I will ascend to heaven," "I will raise my throne," "I will sit enthroned...on the utmost heights," "I will ascend above the tops of the clouds," and "I will make myself like the Most High." He had a plan for himself and a plan for mankind to follow— independence from God the Father.

None of us acts alone. We are not independent of one another. Teenagers typically find a rebellious friend who also desires independence and then act out their rebellion together. Independence feeds rebellion, and the root of it is "I will."

In marriage, it goes something like this—the more of our will, the less of our spouse's will, and ultimately the less of God's will. Rebellion may be found in the heart of a child (see Matt. 10:21), but it never leaves the adult without one's heart and mind being renewed. As adults, we continue in our rebellion against God by thinking that life is all about us and our choices, our decisions. If we desire an illicit relationship, we independently make the choice to rebel against the boundaries of our heavenly Father.

Take a break to communicate. Answer the following questions together:

1. Can you remember feeling any rebellion in your heart against your parents when you were a teenager, still living under their rules? Can you remember

who or what was influencing you at that time of your life? Can you remember any specific examples where you acted on that feeling of rebellion?

2. Can you think of any "I will" moments within your marriage when you were not open to your spouse's opposing view or input?

3. Does independence rise up within you when an authority figure requires you to do something a certain way? Why or why not?

THE RENEWED MIND IS THE BEST COMMUNICATOR

Living in a Genesis 3 world and in a culture that reinforces that world actually promotes the self-centeredness of life as we know it. I (Steve) was standing in line at our local bank one day when in boredom I decided to read a few of the posters on the wall. One in particular caught my eye. It said, "We're not tellers, we're listeners." It's rare to find natural listeners. When we do, we usually take advantage of them. Counselors are inundated with clients who want to be heard. The fact that counselees will pay hundreds of dollars for an hour of counseling time proves our point. People pay inordinate sums of money to be listened to, and when they leave they feel better. Why? Because someone took the time to listen to them and perhaps even repeated back to them what he or she was hearing, proving the need for highly paid listening skills.

But most of us are not natural listeners; most of us would rather talk. Public speaking courses are offered at nearly every college, but have you ever heard of a public listening course? We doubt anyone would ever sign up, even if one were offered. Our point is that listening is a developed skill and one that does not come naturally. It takes a renewed mind transformed by a supernatural God to truly develop both sides of the communication coin. It means being willing to forgo independence to become dependent upon God and interdependent with our spouse and others.

Jesus often repeated the words, "Not my will but my Father's will be done." He told those arguing with Him one day that He only does what the Father tells Him to do. In other words, *if you don't agree with what I say or do, take it up with my Father in heaven, because that's whom I am listening to.* Jesus operated out of a renewed mind, a mind that was transformed from this world to the world of His Father's voice. He had many voices demanding His attention, perhaps every minute of the day, but there was one voice that He had to hear. He often took time to pray and listen for that voice.

THAT STILL, SMALL VOICE

Many years ago, we felt that we heard the voice of our heavenly Father telling us to leave our jobs, our local church, our relationships, and our state to move to northern Pennsylvania to help start a group home for adjudicated delinquent males. It was a huge step of faith to load up our moving truck and drive ten hours north to a very rural, mountainous region. Steve's dad vehemently disagreed with what we were doing. He said we were "throwing our lives away." Mary's parents were ecstatic because they always wanted missionaries in the family. The next eight years of service were a huge growing experience for us personally, for our marriage, and for our leadership skills.

Along with several other dedicated staff members, we knew we had heard God and obeyed Him. He honored that obedience with both great reward and great pain, causing great growth. We never regretted taking that step, but it just didn't make any worldly or natural sense. There was no opportunity for financial wealth; in fact, it was the opposite. There was no opportunity for climbing the corporate ladder. The only ladders we climbed were to paint the barn or replace a leaking roof. It was hard work, pure and simple, but we were there as a couple in agreement, fulfilling a call from heaven. It took transformed minds to hear that still, small voice, to obey the call, and then to stick with the call until we would hear something different eight years later.

Another example of obedience to this still, small voice is close friends of ours who were ready to retire. They had made plenty of money through numerous successful businesses. The options before them were plentiful and possibly exotic. They could live anywhere in the world they desired to begin a life of retirement and ease. However, their transformed minds heard the voice of their heavenly Father. Together, they chose to move to a depressed area of their state and began to take long and consistent prayer walks on the streets of their community. They positioned themselves to reach out to the city officials and get to know them on a personal level. A small group of believers and seekers began fellowshipping together and, in time, a house church was born in this very rural and traditionally religious community. In time, the mayor of their city became a believer through their efforts of obedience. This couple never retired to that life of ease. They heard from heaven, and their spirits were in tune with His Spirit. Through transformed thinking, they did what wealthy retired persons would not naturally do and found supernatural ministry in their later years.

A NATURALLY SUPERNATURAL MIND

A natural mind that is disciplined to hear supernatural thoughts through one's spirit will believe differently and eventually think differently. The Pharisees were continually confronting Jesus concerning His words and actions. Their spirits were not in tune with God's Spirit and consequently failed to see or hear His message. The book of James provides some insight into this very real issue. Chapter 3 presents two types of wisdom—"earthly" and "spiritual." The end result of earthly wisdom is selfish ambition, disorder, and every evil practice (see James 3:16). But heavenly wisdom is pure and peace-loving; it's considerate and full of mercy. The end result of heavenly wisdom is peace and righteousness (see James 3:17-18).

While there seems to be no end to reasons for a marriage to break up today, we believe that the foundation of most of those reasons is selfishness, as James mentioned when he wrote of earthly wisdom. We want what we want. When we live in selfish ambition, we live in a world desiring independence that is controlled by our sinful nature and desires.

When our minds are controlled by the Spirit of God, however, we will submit to God's voice, and our thoughts and actions will be full of life (see Rom. 8:6). The reality of what we are conveying is that according to Romans 8, the transformed mind occurs as the Holy Spirit in our spirit speaks to our mind and not our mind speaking to or directing our spirit. Paul said it well when he wrote, "You, however, are controlled not by the sinful nature but by the Spirit, if the Spirit of God lives in you" (Rom. 8:9). The natural mind controlled by the Spirit of God will believe differently, think differently, feel differently, and behave differently.

A transformed mind listens to the life-giving Holy Spirit and in a brand-new way begins to hear the truth, believe the truth, and speak the truth. That truth revealed by the Spirit is full of grace, speaks in love, is not argumentative, does not have to have its own way, is not rude, is not easily angered, and is patient (see 1 Cor. 13). As these attributes become part of our transformed spirit, they will eventually become part of our transformed minds. From our heart to our mind, we will begin to respond to our spouse with those same attributes.

First Corinthians 13 Exercise

Take the time to read First Corinthians 13 together, and then answer the following questions:

1. Verses 1–3 state that love has to be the core of everything we do. How does a mind not regenerated

by the Spirit of God reflect selfishness? How does a mind renewed by the Spirit reflect love and selflessness?

2. How do the attributes mentioned in verses 4–7 contribute to communication out of a transformed mind?

3. What attributes do I need to ask God for in order to better reflect His love to my mate?

THE MEMORY MINEFIELD

How do we transition from the natural mind to the supernatural mind? Let us share with you what several have called "the memory minefield." Someone once said to us, "I don't know which hurts more, my memories or my spouse." We move forward through life continually looking backward. Every day our thoughts are filled with what happened in the past, and we make decisions based upon that history. In counseling, we have often found that it's not our mate who is hurting us; it's our memory minefield.

Minefields are fields where we have buried or hidden devices (memories) just below the surface. Each of us has memories that can be triggered when we find ourselves in a similar situation to one we may have experienced in the past. It is a form of mental association and can help us recognize when danger may lurk ahead. Based upon past experiences and memories of those experiences, we may love dogs or be afraid of them. If we suffered a traumatic dog attack in which we were bitten, the emotional response will be fear. If our history tells us dogs are full of love and make great companions, we'll experience positive feelings of affection.

How does this affect marriage? Most of day-to-day life is not filled with new revelation but memory. Memory helps you to drive home at the end of your workday; it's what keeps that list of errands you need to run in the back of your mind; and it allows you to remember things about your marriage, such as your anniversary or your spouse's birthday. Think of a life lived without the ability to recall even the most mundane details, let alone the important ones, such as who your friends and family are. It would be disastrous.

When we have an issue in our marriage relationship, we quickly go to our memory bank and pull up a pleasant experience (full of good memories), a neutral experience (full of neither good nor bad emotions, perhaps indifferent), or a negative experience (memories that are painful). When we connect to the pleasant memories, our heart rate is steady and we tend to be at ease, truly embracing the moment with joy. When a negative, pain-filled memory is brought to the surface, our heart rate can increase, we can begin to sweat, and a flood of negative emotions begin to fill our mind.

The problem is that not all of our memories are filled with truth; in fact, quite a large amount of research has shown that they are almost never 100 percent accurate. How you remember an incident and how your spouse remembers the same incident can be two very different observations. My (Steve's) sister and I grew up in the same home with the same parents. But today, when we recall specific historical incidents, it's amazing how different our memories of an incident can be. We remember what stood out to us, and, right or wrong, that was how we perceived it at the time. We've come to accept that we must allow for differences in our memories because our personal view of what happened is filtered differently.

Some of our memories contain lies or curse-filled words that others or even we ourselves have spoken. Though these memories are from life experiences that may have occurred years or even decades ago, they have the power to feel like they happened yesterday. Also, our brains can inadvertently miss important details, rendering the memory inaccurate. Returning to the dog illustration above, our fear of dogs may be based on a single, powerfully negative experience from our past. Today, however, that one historical experience recreates the emotions of fright and flight when we encounter any dog, even though the dog may be the sweetest creature on earth.

It was not uncommon for John and Elizabeth (not their real names) to experience knock-down, drag-out arguments. In sheer frustration late one evening, John looked at Elizabeth and said, "That's it; I'm out of here!" Immediately, Elizabeth went silent and fell to the floor in a fetal position, where she sobbed uncontrollably. Even though John ran immediately to his wife, knelt beside her, and desperately tried to console her, it was as if he had left. Elizabeth didn't or couldn't hear his voice or acknowledge his presence. John later discovered that when his wife was six years old, she overheard her parents fighting. Her father's words rang out as he screamed, "That's it; I'm out of here!" Elizabeth never saw her father again.

John was not her father; he was her dedicated husband. However, when Elizabeth heard that same phrase, she immediately associated the words with her father's words from her childhood. That former experience was automatically connected to the present experience. The characters were different, but in her mind the outcome would be the same. The deep, wrenching pain of loss she once associated with her father's abandonment returned as if it was programmed for this exact moment. Everything in her being was telling her, "Now my husband is leaving me, too." The pain was unbearable, and those same feelings of abandonment returned with a vengeance.

Elizabeth was no longer fighting with John; she was wrestling with pain-filled memories planted in a minefield just below the surface. Was it the argument they needed to resolve, or was it Elizabeth's past hurts that needed to be healed? From many stories like this one, we have come to believe that most relationship issues in the present have a connection to the past; therefore, what seem like marital issues are often individual issues. We are convinced that when Jesus heals our individual issues, sins, hurts, and disappointments, marriage relationship issues can also be healed.

QUESTIONS TO CONSIDER

1. Can you relate to John and Elizabeth's story? Has a personal memory surfaced through a disagreement with your spouse, and can you share how that experience connected to a personal memory?

2. Are there landmines (memories) just below the surface that you avoid at all costs? Can you label them? (For example, the landmine of feeling out of control or the landmine of failure.)

3. Take some time to share how memory can be both a gift and a pain-filled experience. Can you give examples of both?

4. Look up First Corinthians 2:16 and ask yourselves how this scripture relates to the memory minefield.

HEALING HURTS BELOW THE SURFACE

Sometimes the military approaches a minefield using detonation to clear the area from danger. They find the mines and safely set them off, exploding them into the air. At other times, they defuse the detonators one by one so that the mines become harmless. We have similar options. The Holy Spirit can take us to that minefield of memories and help us defuse the mines without exploding and hurting those we love.

Romans 12:2 admonishes us to be transformed by the renewing of our minds. A renewed mind is experiencing the mind of Christ. The mind of Christ is available to us as the Holy Spirit brings healing to memories that are filled with pain and lies. How does He do that? In John 8:32, He tells us that if we hold to His teachings, which are truth, the truth will set us free. If the truth sets us free, then the lies from our past must bind us. Jesus' truth brings freedom from our past to our present and future.

We must seriously and boldly ask Jesus to speak truth to us where we have believed a lie from our past. One day while counseling with Jeff, he revealed to us that when he was growing up, he felt as though he could never please his father. He always felt as though he never measured up to his father's expectations. We asked him if he felt he had his father's approval today, as a married man with children. We were reasonably sure that we knew what his answer would be. Jeff looked at us with a question on his face and said, "No, no I don't."

We will never forget that session with Jeff. We asked Jesus to come to him and reveal His truth to this man who had ached for approval for so many years. Jesus did that, but quite differently than we expected. Jeff saw a picture of himself at home plate on a baseball field, holding a bat and waiting for the pitch from the pitcher's mound. He expected to swing and miss and then hear words of disapproval. Instead, Jeff kept hearing words of approval like, "Good swing, son," "Way to go, you almost got that one," and "Aren't we having fun together?" These were words of affirmation that Jeff had never heard when playing ball with his dad. When Jeff looked up to see who the pitcher was, he couldn't believe what he saw—Jesus was the pitcher.

Today, Jeff tells us that he is healed of the pain found within those particular childhood memories. He now knows he is no longer rejected. When Jeff received the revelation of his heavenly Father's approval, he found all the approval he ever needed for his past, his present, and his future.

In order to know freedom in your marriage, you need to pursue and know individual freedom. As we allow the Holy Spirit into the sewers of our hearts and minds, we are, in effect, asking Him to reveal the hurts that we keep trapped below the surface. If we take those hurts into marriage, they will surface at the wrong time and perhaps toward the wrong person. Personal freedom from past hurts is vital if we desire to experience a marriage not held captive by our past. The goal of this chapter has been to provide healing from our past so that we can clearly move into the future together, unhindered by lies that were once found and held within our memories.

We love and live by this particular verse found in God's Word: "It is for freedom that Christ has set us free" (Gal. 5:1). For no other reason does Christ want you to be free other than to experience personal freedom.

CLOSING QUESTION

Do you agree with the statement that most marriage issues are from individual issues and that as we pursue individual healing our marriage can receive healing? Why or why not?

Chapter Six

MARRIAGE HAS A MISSION

*Sometimes the shortest distance between two
points is a winding path walked arm in arm.*
—ROBERT BRAULT

*Most men love the word "submission" until they
discover it's their responsibility to define the mission.*
—THE AUTHORS

Have you ever been to an ox pull? We were in New England, seated
on a set of old wooden bleachers at a county fair; we had never
experienced a real, live ox pull. Let us try to describe it to you: two
mammoth oxen are yoked together, side by side, and behind them is
an apparatus like a hitch. The hitch is connected to a large chunk of
concrete weighing thousands of pounds. The oxen are commanded
by their owner (called a driver) to pull together and drag the concrete slab as far as they possibly can. It was quite entertaining, and
we immediately began to realize something with the teams of oxen.
Some were young and inexperienced. Some pairs were noticeably different sizes. Some simply refused to work with their partner. But those
teams that were mature and experienced knew how to work together,
with their driver shouting out commands at their sides. Those teams,
we noticed, pulled the heavy concrete a lengthy distance.

We found ourselves thinking about how the teams of oxen were a picture of marriage—specifically, the picture of a team of two either working together successfully or failing miserably to pull in unison. It was not the biggest or strongest team that won; it was the oxen that could work together, each performing to the best of its ability. Working alone, the block wouldn't move an inch; but working in complete harmony, the teams would succeed in reaching the goal.

It astounds us to discover how many couples do not know why they are married. This is the question this chapter will probe—what is your mission together as a couple? For what reason(s) has God called you together into this union? Those who once were two have been called to move as one. When the two oxen didn't compete with one another and acted as one, they were surprisingly successful.

Businesses, civic organizations, churches, and the military all have mission statements. If they understand this statement and what goals are to be accomplished, all of the members or employees of these organizations know why they belong. Mission statements are composed of descriptive terms like "to serve the homeless of our city," "to build a better and more efficient home," or "to protect our nation's borders." When God created man, He also created a mission for man. God gave Adam and Eve an assignment from heaven—to tend the Garden of Eden and to rule over creation.

This assignment was not just busy work; it was a charge from God to care for God's creation and to replenish the earth. There was purpose, a co-mission in this first marriage, and Adam and Eve went about each day fulfilling that call of God upon their lives. Both you and your spouse can discover your co-mission, just like Adam and Eve. You each have both spiritual and natural gifts that balance and complement. As husband and wife, you are a team, yoked together to fulfill all that the Father has planned for you. Perhaps God has called you to the business realm, to be in worship ministry together, or to raise your children and to pay off your mortgage early. All of these can become pieces of your mission together as a married couple.

Life can get busy and pass us by rather quickly. Before we know it, we've been married for five or even ten years. We can begin to myopically focus on the stuff of life that has no real or eternal value or lasting effect upon our lives and the lives of others. It's important to remember why God called you together in matrimony, and writing your mission statement as a couple can help to refocus your marriage on the things that truly matter.

WHERE IT ALL BEGAN FOR US

When Mary and I first discovered the idea of mission as a couple, we were already many years into our marriage. Looking back over several decades, we realized that our first co-mission assignment came from our local church. Our pastor asked us if we would consider starting a bus ministry. The idea was to fill a bus with unchurched kids and bring them to Sunday school. We loved visiting the kids and their families every Saturday and picking them up in our red-and-white converted school bus early Sunday morning. Sometimes they ran to the bus half-dressed due to a lack of parental involvement, but they were excited nonetheless. The bus ministry was so successful that we began a second route, and then a third. Soon we were reaching the parents as well as the children and were helping to grow a multicultural fellowship.

Some years later, we would help to direct a foster children's home for adjudicated delinquent teenagers. Then we began to give birth to our own children, changed jobs, moved, saved money, and built a home—all ingredients of our mission together. We soon discovered many other areas of married life that sealed our reasons for marriage and confirmed why God chose Steve to have a teammate called Mary.

Every time we facilitate premarital counseling, we share the principle of two individual missions merging into one co-mission as the couple is called to marriage. One particular couple found their life missions as individuals to be so opposite that we sent them away to think and pray more deeply about their future together, asking themselves how they would reconcile the differences. As they took several weeks to process what they individually felt God was asking of them for their futures, they found the differences to be too great. Both were unwilling to compromise what they sensed was God's direction for them as singles. They parted before saying "I do" and found tremendous peace in their decision.

Have you ever observed an athletic team that simply could not flow together? Sometimes, rather than opposing the other team, in effect, they oppose themselves. It's a recipe for disaster. As husband and wife, you are not opponents; you are on the same side. Teammates don't place impossible demands upon one another; they look for the strengths of each player so they can effectively make use of those strengths as a team. Being on the same side, you do not sabotage each other's efforts but agree on how to serve together.

For reflection as a couple, discuss the following questions:

1. Like the oxen, in what areas do we find ourselves pulling together to reach a common goal?

2. Are there any areas where we find ourselves pulling at a different pace or resisting the pull of our spouse?

TEAMMATES

Teammates provide a sounding board of encouragement; they believe in each person who makes up their team. One teammate dare not express to another a negative message like, "When you're up to bat, we know you're going to strike out." It's just not part of a healthy game. If it is, you're defeated before you begin, and the coaching staff has missed some valuable team-building principles.

Teammates work with each other's weaknesses rather than exposing them. Teammates are teachable and accountable to one another;

they are individually aware of the fact that they do not know it all. Teammates have high expectations of each other, but they are expectations that they also have of themselves. And teammates believe in one another, even when mistakes are made and they struggle to believe in themselves.

In the movie *Remember the Titans*, Denzel Washington acts out the true story of a football coach in the southern US at a recently desegregated high school. He must find a way to successfully integrate his players in order to become a winning team. In the beginning, the players are not pulling together; instead, they're fighting one another over their racial differences. In a desperate attempt to help his team understand the importance of unity, the coach takes them to Gettysburg, Pennsylvania to teach them about the Civil War. On an early-morning run to a historical battlefield, he explains that the battle to overcome their racial divide has already been fought and decided. It's a powerful word picture, and the team receives the message. Cohesiveness begins to grow, and they begin to win games, becoming a collective force to be reckoned with.

Openly discuss the following questions concerning teamwork:

1. As teammates, in what areas do we find ourselves encouraging one another and supporting one another's weaknesses?

2. Are there any areas where we find ourselves battling one another rather than battling a problem area together?

3. How can we strengthen the quality and depth of our marriage team?

QUALITIES OF A SUCCESSFUL MARRIAGE TEAM

The following are some qualities that we feel will help strengthen your marriage team and fulfill your co-mission. We will also thoroughly address God's government within marriage. This teaching alone can bring tremendous freedom, unity, and purpose to your marriage future.

1. Collaboration

Collaborative teammates do more than just work with one another; each person brings something to the table that adds value to the relationship and synergy to the team. To collaborate is "to work, one with another; to cooperate." Synergy is "the combined action of two or more substances or agents to achieve an effect greater than that which each individually could achieve"—sounds a lot like marriage.

Team members can never have the perspective of looking out for only themselves. The leader of the family is not free to do whatever he/she wants but rather is the one who surrenders his/her freedom to make sure his household is protected and cared for. The lead position is not a position of ease but the position of greatest responsibility.[1] If as a husband we say we cannot change the baby's diaper because we're too busy watching the game, what we're really saying is that our personal agenda is more important than our wife and child.

There are many gifted football players who are not gifted collaborators. Their attitude toward collaboration sounds something like this: *I don't need the team as much as the team needs me. In fact, I am the team, and without me, this team does not exist.* To put it into marriage terms, this would be like saying, "I don't need this marriage, but my husband/wife needs me to help him/her succeed in life."

Mary and I collaborate by drawing upon one another's strong points and strengthening one another's weaknesses. Physically, Mary is often my eyes because I have had numerous eye surgeries; I am often her ears because she suffers from a hearing loss in one ear. Together, we work toward a win-win outcome. In counseling, Mary provides those insights of "being," the heart, insights that often escape me, while I tend to bring the practical side of "doing," the hands-on conflict resolution.

Can you share an example of collaboration from your marriage?

_____

_____

_____

_____

_____

_____

_____

_____

_____

_____

_____

2. *Selflessness*

> *Do nothing out of selfish ambition or vain conceit, but in humility consider [your spouse as] better than yourselves. Each of you should look not only to your own interests, but also to the interests of [your spouse]* (Philippians 2:3-4).

Marriage is about serving one another harmoniously. Great teams help carry one another. Truth be told, my wife is the greatest servant in our relationship. I am not afraid to admit that. I wish I could say that our marriage has always been like a figure skating pair that moves together in synchronized motion throughout its routine, but that routine lasts but a few short minutes while marriage is a lifelong commitment.

Early on in our marriage, I was working and going to graduate school, both full time, while Mary was left to run the household, raise two active boys, give birth to our third child, proofread and type all of my papers, and balance the budget—not an easy job description. However, she did all of it without complaint. Her selflessness was exemplified in her sacrifice for her husband's goal.

Selflessness requires being a giver without posturing oneself in such a manner as to receive all of the benefits. Serving is about interdependence, not independence. Interdependence means we make decisions together and share the weight of responsibility, failure, and success. A great marriage team faces the trials, draws closer to God and one another, and becomes stronger as a team. When a football coach wants to build a great team, he doesn't send them out onto the field to run into pillows and jump on mattresses; they run strenuous, sweat-producing exercises. God does the same with us—He has us face tough opponents like illness, debt, difficulties raising teenagers, and unexpected transitions, and He has us do it together. Whether we grow closer together or fall apart is up to us. "For our struggle is not against flesh and blood," but against evil spiritual forces (Eph. 6:12).

Can you describe a time when you noticed your spouse acting in selflessness?

_____

_____

_____

_____

_____

_____

_____

_____

---

3. Tenacity

To be tenacious is to be steady, to hold firm, to be persistent. It requires 100 percent. Tenacious people do not give up; there is no surrender in tenacity. Mary said to me in complete frustration one day, "Ugh, you are so tenacious!" She didn't mean it as a compliment, but I took it as one because tenacity pushes through adversity until the answer comes. It is running with perseverance: "Let us run with perseverance the race marked out for us" (Heb. 12:1). The Bible says that perseverance is a work that must be finished in us so that we may be mature and complete, not lacking anything (see James 1:4).

When there is an issue between Mary and me, I cannot wait to resolve it, talk about it, and look for a solution. I don't want it hanging in the air or growing, and I don't like tiptoeing around it. But I have to be careful that my tenacity does not turn into pushing or forcing Mary to respond before she's ready. Teams that incorporate tenacity must also incorporate grace (divine love, good will) for each team member. If we do not include grace, we will frustrate our teammate and they may begin to give up, feeling as though they'll never reach the expectation. Together with grace, teams must persevere to the end.

How is tenacity both a positive and a negative within your marriage relationship?

_____

_____

_____

_____

_____

_____

_____

_____

_____

4. Submission

Addressing mission as a couple would not be complete without addressing the biblical term *submission*. To some, this is a word and action to be avoided. To others, it is a convenient way of getting what they want from another. How do we properly understand this all-important scriptural term? We believe the teaching that follows will bring freedom to you and your marriage and will rid your mind of any negative religious overtone concerning this word. But first, let us ask you a few questions about your concept of the word *submission*.

Write your definition of the word *submission* below:

_____

_____

_____

Do you believe that submission is a biblical term?

_____Yes _____No

Does God still require submission of the wife to the husband today?

_____Yes _____No

Does God require submission of the husband to the wife?

_____Yes _____No

Describe how you would identify the act or the position of submission in your marriage presently:

_____

_____

_____

_____

_____

_____

_____

_____

_____

_____

_____

It was 1975, and Mary's pastor was seated behind his gray, military-style desk with green shag carpet like that found in most rooms of his house. We were in the middle of our one and only premarital counseling session, a few short weeks before our wedding day. In the course of his counsel, he asked Mary if she would "submit to Steve's authority." Mary readily agreed and responded wholeheartedly in the affirmative. There was no teaching, no understanding of this word *submit*, simply a reading of a verse in Ephesians 5. Mary thought, "I have no problem with submission. I love Steve and will agree to his leadership in our marriage." Were we naïve? Yes. Did we have our heads in the clouds, knowing that providing all of the "right" answers would finish our session early? Certainly.

In the years that would follow, God began to give us insight into this very important aspect of marriage called submission. He gave us definition and purpose, a purpose that would honor both male and female roles in our call together. He gave us a love for this act of selflessly serving one another in the same way we discovered Jesus constantly submitting to the will of His Father in heaven over His own will. We long to share these principles with each of you, believing that it will radically alter your view of this godly principle given to us from heaven.

GOD'S GOVERNMENT IN MARRIAGE AND THE VALUE OF SUBMISSION

God has given man authority over the fish of the sea, the birds, and every living creature (see Gen. 1:28). God placed man in the garden to work and care for His creation (see Gen. 2:15). From the beginning, God has established an order to things. He is not without government. Think of what this world would be like without God's management. God's scriptural basis for order in the Christian marriage is found in Ephesians 5:21-33. Please take time to read these scriptures. Write below what is revealed about God's government in these verses:

_____

_____

_____

_____

_____

_____

_____

_____

_____

_____

_____

What is submission? The prefix *sub* means "under." The root word is "mission." Therefore, the literal meaning of *submission* is "to be under the mission." The Greek word for submission in Ephesians 5:21-22 is *hupotasso*. *Hupotasso* is primarily a military term. *Hupo* means "under" and *tasso* means "to arrange." Christ has a mission, so then men are in submission to Christ's mission.

If the husband has a mission, then the wife is in submission to her husband's mission. The man is not more important than the woman, but he is the one responsible before God to be clear about the mission. Men, are you clear on the mission from God for your marriage, for your family, for your ministry, and for your future? If you are not clear, how can your wife be clear in her role of submission?

Does the husband force the submission of the wife? No! It is God who commands, first, "submit to one another" and, second, "wives, submit to your husbands as to the Lord" (Eph. 5:21-22). Both uses of the word imply that the one doing the submitting is choosing to place him- or herself under the authority of another.

"Under" does not mean "less than." Imagine a bridge spanning a river valley. Is the bridge merely a road crossing over the water? If it is, it won't stand for long! An extensive support structure *under* the bridge is essential for it to function. Now imagine a train chugging across a prairie. Can the train go anywhere without a track underneath it? Of course not; one cannot function without the other. There can be no attitude of superiority in the husband or the wife. Both roles are significant. One is not more important than the other, just different. Sometimes we have a tendency to think that the most visible position or the one with the highest level of authority is the most important. However, no army ever won a war with just generals.

Let's look at First Peter 3:1-7 to get a better idea of the structure versus the support structure:

> *Wives, in the same way be submissive to your husbands so*
> *that, if any of them do not believe the word, they may be*

won over without words by the behavior of their wives, when they see the purity and reverence of your lives. Your beauty should not come from outward adornment, such as braided hair and the wearing of gold jewelry and fine clothes. Instead, it should be that of your inner self, the unfading beauty of a gentle and quiet spirit, which is of great worth in God's sight. For this is the way the holy women of the past who put their hope in God used to make themselves beautiful. They were submissive to their own husbands, like Sarah, who obeyed Abraham and called him her master. You are her daughters if you do what is right and do not give way to fear. Husbands, in the same way be considerate as you live with your wives, and treat them with respect as the weaker partner and as heirs with you of the gracious gift of life, so that nothing will hinder your prayers.

According to verse 7, men are to honor women as the weaker vessel. This does not mean the "lesser than" vessel. It does not say that the woman *is weaker* but that we are to honor her *as* the weaker. If there is a *weaker* vessel, there must be a *weak* vessel as well.

God's plan requires the wife to submit and the husband to love. Submitting and loving both require continuous repeated action. God has a government. His management of the male/female role is superior to any other system of management. God's order is to cover everyone through His love. "Now I want you to realize that the head of every man is Christ, and the head of the woman is man, and the head of Christ is God. ...In the Lord, however, woman is not independent of man, nor is man independent of woman. For as woman came from man, so also man is born of woman. But everything comes from God" (1 Cor. 11:3,11-12).

Originally God created woman from man. Now man is born of woman. We are not independent of the other. In God's sight, we are equal. Let's face the facts—without woman, none of us would even be here. We are equal but not the same. "There is neither Jew nor Greek, slave nor free, male nor female, for you are all one in Christ Jesus" (Gal. 3:28). Quite simply, we need one another.

Take the time to answer the following questions:

1. After reading this exercise and studying the Scriptures, how has your view of God's government for a husband and wife changed or been challenged?

2. How would you now rewrite your definition of *submission*?

3. Do either of you need to apologize for any wrong thinking concerning this wonderful gift of God's government?

4. Would you be willing to repent before God right now if there has been any misuse of God's government in your marriage? Consider praying with one another for God to reestablish His blessing of godly government.

Team Mission

Amos 3:3 asks, "Do two walk together unless they have agreed to do so?" Teams figure out what it takes to achieve victory and then do it—this is mission. Teams succeed when there is a unified team mission and a cooperative spirit among team members. As a couple, Mary and I pray about our cooperative mission. We write down aspects of that mission in order to develop our mission statement. We have areas in which we are called to serve as individuals; however, our mission statement expresses our calling from God as a couple.

One key to mission is leadership. Once the mission is recognized, who is ultimately responsible to achieve it? Who has the authority to lead the team in fulfilling its mission? John Maxwell says that leadership is the capacity to translate vision into reality. When leadership is hindered, reaching the goal of the mission will be hindered. Lou Holtz, the great Notre Dame football coach, once said, "You've got to have great athletes to win; I don't care who the coach is. You can't win without good athletes, but you can lose with them. This is where coaching makes the difference."[2]

God's Mission

God had a mission. He sent His Son to earth to bring the life-changing good news of the Kingdom of Heaven while He lived among us (see John 3:16). Jesus Christ also had a mission. He obediently gave His life for all of mankind on the cross of Calvary (see John 6:38). As Jesus would be resurrected and ascend to be with His Father, having finished His mission on the earth, He sent the Holy Spirit to live in us as we would remain, walking out our mission on the earth (see Acts 1:8). All three members of the Trinity—God the Father, Jesus the Son, and the Holy Spirit—had a mission. Adam and Eve were given a mission, as were Moses, Jeremiah the prophet, Paul the apostle, Luke the physician, and so on.

As you look over these six qualities of a successful marriage team, what areas are present in your relationship and what areas need to be strengthened? How will you strengthen the weak areas, and how will you maintain the qualities that presently exist within your relationship?

Steve and I (Mary) appreciate and embrace our mission in marriage together. It has changed over the years from raising our children to caring for elderly parents, but serving together keeps us on track, on point. Never once have I felt "less than" as a wife through this gracious gift called submission. Never once have I been forced into something I did not agree with, because we have listened and prayed together in order to be like that team of oxen who successfully pulls in unison. I can't begin to describe the satisfaction derived in marriage from this one principle. If you'll take the time to discover your mission together, we believe that same satisfaction will be yours as well.

YOUR MISSION STATEMENT

Each of us possesses gifts from God (see 1 Cor. 12:12-20, 27-31; Rom. 12:6-8). With these gifts comes a personal responsibility to use them both individually and in marriage. Begin by listing your personal gifts below; these could include technical skills, physical skills, and/or spiritual skills. Feel free to enlist the help of your mate to identify some of these gifts.

WIFE	HUSBAND
1.	1.
2.	2.
3.	3.
4.	4.
5.	5.

Once your gifts have been listed, move on to list some of the areas in which you are presently involved, both individually and as a couple (e.g., marriage, parenting, community service boards, workplace roles, church responsibilities).

WIFE	HUSBAND
1.	1.
2.	2.
3.	3.
4.	4.
5.	5.

Of all the gifts you have and roles you play, what are you called to for this season of your marriage? As you narrow these areas down, you can begin to write phrases that become mission statements. For example, you may create a phrase that states something like the following: "We are called to love our spouse as Christ loved His church and to nourish our children in the principles of God's Word." You might also include something about your business that reads, "We are committed to running our business through principles of integrity and to growing our company to help meet the needs of our community." For an example of a mission statement, see the paragraph below.

Mission Statement Example

> As a couple, we desire to experience Jesus intimately and to bring the fruit of that relationship to the practical application of our marriage. We desire to raise godly children and to make a deep investment into their lives through mentoring, training, and loving them unconditionally. We desire to retire our mortgage early and to live debt-free in order to be a tool for God's giving, to care for aging parents. We desire to fulfill God's call by serving at our local church, supporting missionaries, sponsoring a child, and praying together regularly.

Take some time now to begin writing out your co-mission statement, including the gifts and areas of involvement you listed above, defining what you are called to as a couple for this season of marriage:

_____

_____

_____

_____

_____

_____

_____

_____

_____

Now that you have crafted your marriage co-mission statement, you can begin writing practical goals that will help to fulfill the statement. For example, if you desire to pay off your home mortgage early, construct a goal that indicates how you will practically accomplish this task, such as limiting dining out in order to pay extra money toward your loan. If a portion of your co-mission is related to raising children, perhaps taking a parenting class would help to fulfill this goal. Take several goals from the mission statement you constructed above; then, make a copy of those goals to pray about together and to serve as a reminder of reaching your co-mission as a team.

Goal:

_____

Objectives to accomplish this goal:

_____

_____

Goal:

_____

Objectives to accomplish this goal:

_____

_____

Goal:

_____

Objectives to accomplish this goal:

_____

_____

Goal:

_____

Objectives to accomplish this goal:

_____

_____

Goal:

_____

Objectives to accomplish this goal:

_____

_____

_____

Finally, no team can neglect the fundamentals, and often maintaining a team means doing some things that we do not like doing. Anything neglected eventually falls apart, rusts, or breaks down. I (Steve) once knew a man who never provided the necessary upkeep to anything he owned. These items, including his house, would eventually decay to the point of disrepair and would deteriorate to the point of no return. What a sad example of waste and loss!

Like the oxen illustration, each team was at a different stage of development, growth, and ability. You could recognize those differences in how successful they were at reaching their goal. As couples, we are growing as a team each passing day, month, and year. Give grace to one another and strive to be teammates who pull and pray together. Discover co-mission as a couple and you'll discover new meaning to your *staying together.*

NOTES

1. Eric and Leslie Ludy, *The First 90 Days of Marriage* (W Publishing Group, 2006) 93.

2. John Maxwell, *The 17 Essential Questions of a Team Player* (Maxwell Motivations, Inc., 2002) 162.

Chapter Seven

FIGHTING AND ARGUING OR PRAYING AND AGREEING

*Kissing is a means of getting two people so close together
that they can't see anything wrong with each other.*
—RENE YASENEK

*Women hope men will change after marriage but they
don't; men hope women won't change but they do.*
—BETTINA ARNDT

We made a major discovery early in our marriage. When it came to conflict, we could choose to "fight and argue," or we could "pray and agree." Disagreement is powerful, but agreement is even more powerful. The Scriptures tell us that if any two persons will agree together in prayer, they will receive what they are asking for (see Matt. 18:19). Let us illustrate.

Our most frequent disagreements focused on the fact that Mary was a "spender" and I (Steve) was a "saver" when it came to our personal view of finances. Those two opposing values would often clash. Truthfully, both views had their positives and their negatives. Serving in missions at the time meant that we had very few resources, but to be honest, we can fight and argue when we have a lot of money or very little money. We had to move beyond right, wrong, and disagreement; we had to move to prayer and asking for God's direction.

During those eight years of mission work, we quickly discovered that we had to stop looking to one another to meet our needs. Neither of us had any money to do so. We lived by faith for our income and had to monitor each and every dollar we came upon. "Tight" could not have begun to describe our financial situation. We were literally dependent upon God for our paycheck. Fighting and arguing was easy because we knew we could blame the other for spending the last bit of cash we had; but it was in this environment that we discovered a scriptural precedent that really helped us, and it's been one we have carried throughout our life together.

At the close of James 3, two types of wisdom are discussed—earthly and heavenly. Earthly wisdom can be full of selfish ambition, but heavenly wisdom is peace-loving and submissive, full of mercy. James 4:1 then asks a very direct and necessary question concerning fights and quarrels and where they come from. James wisely uncovers that at the core of disagreement, we want something but are not getting it. In other words, Steve wants one thing and Mary wants another.

Take a moment to discuss the following questions:

1. Think of your last disagreement, no matter how small or how large. At its core, did one of you desire one thing and the other something different? Without rehashing the conflict, try to remember what the two dissimilar desired outcomes were.

2. Now that you have identified the two desired outcomes, what needs were you each attempting to meet? Again, please do not put yourselves back in the disagreement; this is merely an exercise for learning and application for the future.

A Scriptural Answer Concerning Conflict

The answer given in James 4:2 is to ask God for what you need, without selfish motives, rather than demanding it from each other. James simply says to pray instead of fighting and arguing. What a novel idea—ask God, and stop demanding from your life mate. In the above answers to the questions, can you remember praying and asking God for an answer rather than fighting and arguing?

We discovered as we learned to pray first that God enabled us to see our partner's view more quickly. He helped us to move toward wanting to bless the other rather than withholding and remaining selfish. He helped us to see that our use of the terms "spender" and "saver" were terms of critical judgment that became negative to us. Instead, He gave us new and far more positive language for our differences. Mary was actually a "giver" and I was more of an "investor" for future needs.

Any two persons can disagree at times; it's natural. In fact, it would be unnatural *not* to have disagreements. When we deeply love someone or care about someone, our disagreements can be even more intense due to the fact that we have so much invested in the relationship. We each have our perspective, our filters, and our view through the lens of our histories, experiences, life training, families of origin, and fears. Disagreement in a relationship is not the problem; staying in the mode of disagreement or fighting is. We must stop long enough to discern what it is we need and then find the solution to reach agreement concerning those needs.

At the core of disagreement is the attainment of a need, and sometimes it's the attainment of a mere want. Either way, we want to be sure that you receive this profound message: it is not disagreement itself that is the problem. Rather, it's the inability to resolve disagreement. Social scientists tell us that the biggest predictor of whether a marriage will make it is whether the individuals in the marriage possess an ability to resolve a conflict by finding a solution both can embrace.

Many years ago, we discovered that we could sit across from a couple in an attempt to counsel them and listen to the "problems" in their marriage for hours. It was not unusual to keep hearing the "he said/she said" phrases like we were listening to a broken record. In our later years, we became a bit wiser and requested the couples come to their first counseling appointment with a list of solutions they had already attempted in an effort to resolve the problems. Then, we required each of them to write down what they perceived being the solutions to the problems.

This seemingly small change made an incredible difference in those first sessions. It required the couples to begin thinking about what had not worked and then think about what might work to resolve their issues. Those couples or individuals who did not complete the assignment quickly discovered that their unwillingness to even look toward a possible solution was prolonging the problems. They preferred to fight in an attempt to "win" the argument.

Unfortunately, we must let you in on a little secret—if one spouse "wins," meaning the other loses, they both lose. Because we are one flesh, the goal is a win/win rather than a win/lose situation. Consider the following:

1. Go back to your responses to the two questions above. Can you recall your agreed-upon solution? Did one of you win, in reality meaning that both of you lost?

2. How can we move toward a greater level of agreement and find solutions that are a win/win for us rather than a win/lose (in effect, lose/lose)?

RESISTANCE

When conducting couples' retreats and seminars across the country and in other nations, we often stop and ask the couples to stand

and face one another. We then ask the woman and the man to raise their right hands and place them palm to palm. The next piece of instruction is very important—we ask the woman to push against her husband's palm. Invariably, even though we gave no instruction for the men to push back, they do. Why? We naturally resist when placed under pressure.

The women are simply following instructions, but at the same time they could be thinking, "I am going to resist his resistance because I am not going to be overpowered by him!" Meanwhile, the men are thinking, "I don't know what kind of game this is, but I'm going to win" or "If she pushes me, I push back." Many of us have been pushing back all of our married lives. It's time to stop pushing and start looking for solutions together.

Paul the apostle wrote in Romans 7 that we naturally resist, and even in our desire to do good we often encounter trouble carrying it out. We want to do good, but we struggle with another law that resides within us—an opposing war within (see Rom. 7:14-25).

What is at the core of our resistance? Some of us love and embrace change, but most of us actually resist change in our lives. For some, a change as simple as moving the couch to the other side of the room can create discomfort. For others, to not move the couch on a regular basis causes life to become boring, too predictable.

We have a four-lane highway near our home on which the speed limit is 65 miles per hour. There are often newspaper articles detailing drivers who are caught speeding in excess of 85 miles per hour. Occasionally, when there is a construction sign up and the speed limit is adjusted to 45, it seems that very few can remain within the limit. The drivers are so used to speeding that 45 miles an hour feels torturous to them. Unless the drivers are convinced there is sufficient evidence to make a change, and that change will in some way will benefit them, they will stick with the status quo because it feels comfortable.

Even change for the good can be a subject of resistance for us. Resistance is not necessarily rational, especially when it becomes an issue of power and control. For example, some teenagers live in resistance to anything and everything. It's a season of life in which they are testing their environment; thus, some teenagers encounter numerous driving issues such as speeding tickets and accidents.

As a parent, I (Steve) discovered that I could respond to my children with the answer "no" just because their request represented change or something different from what I interpreted to be the norm. One day when he was young, our oldest son asked to take a bath upstairs rather than his regular shower in the bathroom downstairs. I found myself forming the word "no" with my lips, when I realized that I was preparing to say no just because it was out of sync with the norm. There was absolutely no other reason to say no to him. Mid-word, I changed my answer to "yes" and then said, "Grab your towel from the shower downstairs and go ahead and enjoy your bath." I have no idea why he wanted to take a bath instead of a shower, but he never asked to do so again. I almost prevented something so simple just because his request did not fit the everyday routine. How strange and resistant we are sometimes when it comes to a change of routine.

Famed preacher Charles Swindoll was once asked the question, "If you could raise your children over again, what would you do differently?" His answer: "I would say yes more." Resisting change will keep that little, single syllable word "no" on our lips continually.

Answer the following:

1. Do you sometimes say the word "no" just because saying "yes" represents something different than expected?

2. How can we say "yes" more often, even when it means a change for us?

3. How can the two of you help one another to identify areas of resistance in your lives?

4. What steps can you take to listen and consider a voice that speaks something different from what we are thinking without initially resisting?

KEEPING GRACE IN PLACE AND MOVING BEYOND RESISTANCE

Leadership roles, power issues, and change do not threaten a healthy couple. They don't need to fear differences of opinion or change. They have learned to make the necessary adjustments at appropriate times. When life is out of control, such as during the loss of a job, they understand that change is inevitable and begin to prepare to embrace what lies ahead.

Both husband and wife are called to be leaders in the home. There is not a unilateral leadership plan, as we each have different roles and both are necessary. Husband and wife are called to serve, and that takes grace-filled flexibility. Further, it is not healthy to have one of us doing all the initiating and all the decision-making while one partner just tags along. It is not a competition to see who can make the most changes but rather an identifying of key roles for each of us.

When grace and a heart to serve are present, we stop competing for our needs and start adjusting our roles in the home to best suit our gifts and talents. Of the two of you, who is better at financial or organizational skills? Who is more knowledgeable about home repair or car maintenance? When you make these discoveries, resistance can dissipate, and you can hand over authority in those areas willingly. The more secure we become in our own roles, the more we can trust in our partner's abilities and roles. The more trust we find, the less resistance we encounter.

At one time, Steve handled all of our finances, but today I (Mary) handle them, including filing multiple types of taxes. Remember the "saver" and "spender" issue we had? Why would anyone in their right mind place the "spender" in charge of the finances? What happened? Over time, as we stopped resisting one another, we began to see how our different approaches to financial resources could actually be a gift to our marriage. It didn't happen overnight, but by continually praying about our differences instead of arguing, we began to adapt and embrace what we each uniquely brought to the marriage.

For further discussion:

1. Discuss an issue from your past together that felt overwhelming. Does it still affect you today? If so, how might you need to adjust to find a solution that works for both of you? If not, how did you resolve it?

2. How can you affirm the gifts that you each uniquely bring to the marriage?

3. Share any observed areas where one or both of you freely adapted to the way of your mate.

4. What new roles can you encourage in one another? In appointing roles and responsibilities in your relationship, make sure one of you does not get all the "grunt" jobs while the other the "glamor" jobs.

5. Pray together about your roles and how you can each become a better leader in both individual and shared areas of responsibility.

MOVING TOWARD RESOLUTION

Despite what you may think, conflict is one of our best opportunities for growth as partners. When we push through an opposing force in a healthy way, we grow, change, become stronger and more confident. You can never climb a mountain and at the top say, "I wish it wouldn't have been so steep or so tough." It's that very steepness and toughness that make climbing mountains rewarding; otherwise, few would actually appreciate it. Never promise someone that marriage will be easy. There are some tough climbs, but as we resolve issues, we become stronger, closer, and more confident in our oneness. Many couples miss out on the results of resolving conflict. They get stuck at the fighting and arguing stage and never reach the summit—prayer and agreement.

In our desire to find answers to our differences, we stumbled upon a seven-step process. We want to share that process with you now and expose one of our own disagreements.

After completing eight years of serving as missionaries, I (Steve) was now employed full time as a social worker with a real-life paycheck, albeit a small one. Mary was working full time at home with our three children. At the same time, I was in graduate school full time, and Mary was editing, proofing, and typing my papers on an old Olivetti typewriter. (We did not have the money to purchase a computer or a word processor at the time. If I remember correctly, we paid $100 for the typewriter, which can still be found in our attic.)

Mary now had the enjoyment of going to the store for groceries and actually spending money. I, to my own personal embarrassment, would ask her about the grocery items and why we needed certain ones. Even worse, I would go over the receipt to see what items we could have eliminated in order to spend less. While we had left missions, the mentality of missions had not left us. We actually encountered what we now refer to as a "spirit of poverty" rather than generosity.

Let us share with you our seven steps[1] along with some illustration for each step:

1. *Understand/Identify*

Recognize that any two individuals will come into conflict from time to time. Identify what the conflict is, and then identify each person's understanding of the problem as well as the feelings generated from this conflict. Remember, there are three sides to every story—yours, theirs, and somewhere in the midst of it all, the truth. "The first to present his case seems right, till another comes forward and questions him" (Prov. 18:17). Sometimes Mary and I were so busy trying to get our point across that we didn't stop to hear our spouse's point or need. We desired to be understood more than to understand each other.

2. Set Aside Time

Set aside time to deal with the conflict. When emotions are out of control, take time to step back, calm down, think and pray, and then come back together. Out-of-control anger will not serve you or your spouse. Proverbs 15:1 has some very sound advice: "A gentle answer turns away wrath, but a harsh word stirs up anger." (The use of a key phrase that signals we will come back together within a specified period of time to deal with the problem can be advantageous at this point, e.g., "We need a cup of coffee.") We often failed to set aside time, as Steve wanted to immediately address the issue, and I (Mary) needed time to think through and process it.

3. Agreement

Discover areas where you are in agreement, not just disagreement. At that point in our lives, the only agreement we could find was that our family needed groceries.

4. Stay on the Subject at Hand

Keep to the immediate conflict; don't allow yourselves to go down a rabbit trail into unrelated areas. Too often, we wander into former conflicts in an attempt to arm ourselves with more ammo for the fight. Proverbs 26:20 says, "Without wood a fire goes out." It's not more wood or ammo we need or to change the subject; we need the tenacity to stay on the subject in order to eventually reveal an agreed-upon resolve. When we go beyond the subject at hand, we become more concerned about winning rather than resolving.

5. Appreciate

Appreciate your spouse's opinion and what they add to the process. When you value the ideas and feelings of your partner, you value that person. We had to develop this appreciation in our conflict. I (Steve) appreciated Mary's desire to care for her family in taking the time to go grocery shopping with a baby and two young children. And I (Mary) appreciated that Steve cared about the bottom line and our financial balance, and I had to realize that he was working hard to be a provider for our family.

6. Identify the Needs

Allow for the needs of each partner to be met. When needs are met, conflict can be resolved. Identify the needs each of you may have that are not being met in the conflict. I (Steve) never identified it, but Mary's need was to stock her shelves; in stocking her shelves with food, she was meeting a need of her family for security. Steve's real need was for me (Mary) to stay within our agreed-upon budget even though I found bargains on a weekly basis. I simply had to rein in that extra spending, even when I thought it would save us money another week. Steve needed to feel that he was a good provider for our family.

7. Explore the Options and Move toward a Solution

There were several options, both plausible and not, that we explored for our situation. We could stop eating. Steve could go for the groceries. (In fact, for a time, he did. He stuck to the list a lot better than I did and actually stayed within the budgeted grocery amount.) Or, we could increase the grocery amount in our budget, and when I spent under that agreed upon amount, I could keep the balance for myself, as I wasn't working outside the home. Do you know what I did with this extra money? I often bought gifts for my family and others. It was so freeing to have my own money in my wallet. It truly met a need that up until this point was not even realized or identified. Searching for the right solution brought resolve to several financial issues we were dealing with at the time.

Do you have to follow every one of these steps every time you have a difference or a difficulty? No, but if you incorporate any number of these steps into your lives and communication, you will discover new patterns of agreement versus disagreement. Proverbs 29 reminds us that a fool gives total vent to his anger and stirs up dissension. Keep in mind First Corinthians 13:5, which reminds us that love is not easily angered and simply does not keep any record of our wrongdoing.

For your review:

1. As you consider the steps above, which ones have you used and which have you often missed?

2. Proverbs 17:9 advocates covering over an offense in order to promote love. How and when should we move toward "covering over" in order to promote love rather than jumping right into an offense (see also Prov. 17:14 and 19:11)?

Someone once said that it is in the difficult times in our lives that we grow the most, not in the easy times. Even if your family of origin did not resolve conflict well, you can. If you will pray, follow the above steps, and listen to each other and God, as well as consider each other's needs, you'll be well on your way to fewer disagreements and more agreement.

NOTE

1. Seven steps of resolving conflict adapted from *Called Together* by Steve and Mary Prokopchak, Destiny Image Publishers.

Chapter Eight

PUTTING YOUR MONEY WHERE YOUR VALUE IS

*Marriage has no guarantees. If that's what you're
looking for, go live with a car battery.*
—ERMA BOMBECK

Marriage is about love; divorce is about money.
—AUTHOR UNKNOWN

*In marriage do thou be wise: prefer the person before
money, virtue before beauty, the mind before the body; then
thou hast a wife, a friend, a companion, a second self.*
—WILLIAM PENN

Financial decisions are value decisions. If you look closely at your monthly bank statements, checkbook, or credit card receipts, it will be easy to determine what you value as a couple. The bottom line is we spend our money according to our values.

Fill in the following chart in order to identify similar or differing financial values.

	HIGHLY VALUE	MODERATE VALUE	LITTLE TO NO VALUE
I VALUE DEBT-FREE LIVING.			
I VALUE FAMILY VACATIONS.			
I VALUE REGULAR ENTERTAINMENT.			
I VALUE EATING OUT.			
I VALUE DEBT FOR ASSET PURCHASES.			
I CAN VALUE DEBT FOR NON-ASSET PURCHASES.			
I VALUE DOING THE BOOKKEEPING.			
I VALUE MAINTAINING A BUDGET.			
I VALUE USING CREDIT CARDS REGULARLY.			
I VALUE USING MOSTLY CASH.			
I VALUE A NEWER CAR.			
I VALUE A GROWING SAVINGS ACCOUNT.			

I VALUE GIVING.			
I VALUE SAVING FOR RETIREMENT.			
I VALUE FINANCIAL ACCOUNTABILITY.			
I VALUE REGULAR FINANCIAL DISCUSSIONS.			
I VALUE NEEDS VS. WANTS.			

What value differences can you identify from the above exercise and how have those differences affected your relationship? How have you been working through those differences in order to find financial agreement? How can you augment your values in order to find agreement?

Mary and I already confessed to you that our biggest disagreements early on in our marriage had to do with money. We talked about our differences in how we valued and viewed finances. But what we didn't discuss was how to make those distinct differences a point of strength rather than a point of weakness within our relationship. Often, right down to the demise of a marriage relationship, we can experience deeply heated and contested issues over money and co-owned possessions.

If your goal was to tear apart your marriage, money arguments would certainly help. But marriage is not about me and mine; it's about us and ours. Too often, couples keep their finances separate, which eliminates an opportunity to increase oneness. Why do so many couples operate this way? Sometimes it's from past hurt and disagreements, but primarily it is a result of distrust. We divide up our finances and consequently divide up our responsibilities. The more we separate ourselves, the more we're challenged to find unity and agreement in all areas of marriage. If we can separate our finances, what other areas will eventually be separate?

I (Steve) was meeting with a very dignified and wealthy older couple one afternoon at my office. That day we were conducting a behavioral personality test, which the couple needed to pay for. After the session, the husband inquired about the cost of the profile. I told him it would be 12 dollars. He looked in his wallet and then turned to his wife and said, "I don't have anything less than a 50-dollar bill; you pay him." After that, he abruptly stood up and walked out the door. His wife looked at me and rolled her eyes as if to say, "He does this all the time." Her nonverbal message spoke volumes about how her husband handled his finances separate from hers over the years.

Questions to consider:

1. Are your finances pooled in a single account so that both of you have equal access, or are they located in separate accounts?

2. If your finances are separate, why are they separate? Is there any distrust or fear present? If so, are there hurts from your past that you need to deal with?

WISDOM

The book of Proverbs is packed full of financial wisdom. Solomon was the wealthiest man of his time and had exceptional wisdom to go along with his financial prowess. Over time, we've been able to locate each verse that connects to the use of money or a financial principle and highlighted it in the Bible. Then, throughout our marriage, we've attempted to incorporate those principles concerning money into our life and beliefs. Within this chapter, we have endeavored to appropriately place those highly valuable scriptures alongside the financial principles we've learned.

There are never any guarantees in life to prosperity, and yet there are biblical principles of wisdom that will help you avoid certain financial disaster. The following principles are not all-inclusive, but we hope they will be as helpful to you in your marriage as they have been to us.

THE STARTING PLACE: GENEROSITY

The place to start is with the topic of generosity, because generosity is an attitude of the heart. At first, perhaps, it is a test of ownership, but as one gives and then continually discovers a return in multiple ways, giving becomes a lifestyle. Generosity is a sign of maturity in a believer's life. Generosity is also highly subjective; Jesus noticed the generosity of the widow placing a mite in the collections. It seems generosity is based more upon what we have left rather than what we give (see Mark 12:43-44). In everything we do, we need to incorporate a spirit of generosity; it is life to others and yourself, i.e., give and it will be given unto you. Proverbs 22:9 says, "A generous man will himself be blessed, for he shares his food with the poor."

Mary is one of the most generous persons I know. She is constantly blessing others with her gift of giving. Sowing into others brings joy to her heart and it's contagious. Wherever I travel, I normally carry a gift from my wife to my host. Her gift giving has helped to open doors for me and to grow relationships. Mary also never seems to run out of resources to share. She trusts in the Word of God, which promises that if we give, it will be given to us, even multiplied.

Giving generously and faithfully is a test of trust. It is acknowledging, as a couple, that God gives us our resources. When we are obedient in giving, He is faithful in provision in numerous ways. Steve and I (Mary) gave our lives to missions for eight years. There was no guarantee of income, and most years we lived well below the poverty line. We were unable to accrue any substantial savings and had no credit in order to borrow from a bank. When we completed the mission work, we needed a home. For a season, we lived in a small, two-bedroom apartment with three children in one bedroom and Steve and I sleeping on the floor in the other.

We loved being together, but it was tight quarters. Real estate agents didn't want to work with us because we had so few resources. Then one day Zada showed up. She was an elderly widow from my home church who supported us while we were missionaries. Zada said, "I'm selling my farm, and I'm allowed to subdivide some lots for building."

Steve looked at her and said, "OK, that's nice."

Zada continued, "The Lord is telling me to give you and Mary one of those lots, an acre." We stared at one another and then back at Zada in disbelief. "You heard me," she said. "Go out to the farm and see where you would like your acre."

We didn't realize that an acre of ground paid in full is great collateral to a bank, but suddenly they were willing to speak with us about a home loan. Zada's gift was the beginning of the miracle that is the house we still live in today. We discovered that God is the greatest real estate agent, the greatest banker, the greatest lawyer, and the greatest homebuilder.

Consider these questions:

1. How do you as a couple decide who to give to or where to give? Are you in agreement with your level of giving?

2. Which one of you tends to be more generous? Have you historically viewed this generosity as a positive or a negative?

ARE YOU AN OWNER OR A STEWARD?

There is a scriptural truth that states God gives us the power and opportunity to create and possess wealth. This confession is where it begins and ends. The scripture reveals, "He did all this so you would never say to yourself, 'I have achieved this wealth with my own strength and energy. Remember the Lord your God. He is the One who gives you power to be successful, in order to fulfill the covenant He confirmed to your ancestors with an oath" (Deut. 8:17-18 NLT).

If God provides for us and shares this wealth with us, then our position before Him is that it is all His, and we simply steward that which He shares with us. When we tithe 10 percent, there is not a remaining 90 percent that is ours. One hundred percent is His. Ten percent to our local church as a tithe is a starting point, our first step of obedience in honoring the One who provides it all. We then sow offerings and firstfruits to others in missions and certain spiritual projects in order to help change lives. "Honor the Lord with your wealth, with the firstfruits of all your crops; then your barns will be filled to overflowing, and your vats will brim over with new wine" (Prov. 3:9-10).

This is the first step in our own financial discipline. It is a step that says Jesus is Lord of our finances. It is caring for the poor and the marginalized. It is saying that our wealth is not ours, but God's, and He can use it for His purposes. "A generous man will prosper; he who refreshes others will himself be refreshed" (Prov. 11:25).

Along with stewardship, remaining accountable with our finances is a key factor for us as couples. First, we are accountable to God and then to one another. Next, we are accountable to provide for our family and to use our finances properly for daily provision. The people who view their finances as "theirs to do with whatever they desire" will most certainly encounter ongoing financial difficulty and disagreement.

Spousal accountability has saved many from a disastrous "sure bet." Solomon wrote that ill-gotten treasures are of no value (see Prov. 10:2). The reason for this lack of value is that they are neither worked for nor earned. When we are repeatedly handed something of value for which we did not labor, we will not appreciate its true worth. This is especially true as we train our children about money, whether through an allowance, a first car, college tuition, or other approach. "Dishonest money dwindles away, but he who gathers money little by little makes it grow" (Prov. 13:11).

Discuss the following questions together:

1. How do you remain accountable to one another with your finances? Is there anyone else outside yourselves to whom you are accountable?

2. Do you agree with the statement that says that 100 percent of our resources belongs to God?

3. If we have developed a pattern of making financial decisions separately from each other, how do we begin to make a change and bring our finances together in unity?

OUR RELATIONSHIP WITH MONEY

Does it sound strange to associate the word *relationship* with the word *money*? There is a very short but meaningful verse found in First Timothy 6:6: "But godliness with contentment is great gain." Many people believe that if they had more money they would be more content. But contentment is a state of the heart, mind, and spirit, not level of income, amount of savings, or accumulation of possessions. To be content is to be satisfied, being at ease of mind. Our relationship with money can bring us to contentment or fleetingly take us to discontentment. It can move us to generosity or bind us into hoarding. It can be of diminutive consideration or we can allow it to literally consume us.

The verse in First Timothy said "godliness" brings contentment, not money or stuff. Paul the apostle once shared that he learned to be content with little or with much. Today our culture trains us in discontentment and then counters with advertisements about *things* that will satisfy. But there is no lasting happiness with things. When we connect happiness with the accumulation of wealth and possessions, our happiness will always be short-lived. The new and improved and more efficient model is just around the corner—then what?

Evaluate your relationship with money:

1. Do you believe that if you had more money, you would be more content?

2. Do you reason that if you had more money, you would be more generous?

3. How do you perceive reaching contentment with little or with much wealth/possession?

VEHICLES FOR BEING IN CONTROL OF OUR MONEY

Budgeting

First and foremost, create a budget. Write down exactly what's coming in and what's going out. A budget is simply a picture of income and expenses. A spreadsheet with figures on it will not keep anyone from spending, but it will show you where your money is going. A budget, if used correctly, can help maintain discipline and provide a picture of where your finances are designated ahead of time. A budget should reflect an entire year, not just one month, because there are numerous annual and semi-annual expenses for which you must account. Remember to be as generous as possible with your family because, "A greedy man brings trouble to his family" (Prov. 15:27).

At the end of this chapter, we include an annual budget sheet with instructions on how to complete it. If you take the time to fill in the blanks, you will discover a tool that helps to move you toward agreement in both your income and expenditures. You will also discover the need for addressing debt, savings, and retirement accounts. Two of the categories that surprise most people who fill out such a comprehensive budget sheet are their miscellaneous category and their gift spending; these categories are easy to overlook but can often account for more spending than we think.

This is the first budget sheet we ever used. For one year we dutifully filled out the income and expense categories each month. It took consistency and tenacity to maintain the practice, but in the end many of our unknown expenses became known, and we then had a more comprehensive picture of our annual budget. We then began to develop financial goals as a couple.

Soon we began to pay off our debt, all the way to making our final mortgage payment. We paid off our 30-year note in 12 years. It wasn't because we were wealthy or had high-paying jobs but because we were faithful to pay extra on the principle of the loan monthly. It was amazing to be in agreement financially and to watch the dollars of debt drop off of the back end of the loan. Through the use of a budget, we found agreement and accountability, and we stuck to it. It wasn't always easy to do without some of life's pleasures that we thought we should be enjoying, but as we look back, the financial freedom we eventually found was worth it.

A completed and followed budget sheet helped us to work at making financial decisions ahead of time as much as is possible. So many purchases are emotional or spontaneous and not well thought out, especially with the availability of a credit card. A good rule of thumb with certain purchases is to wait to purchase the item for one month; if you still need it and have the finances designated after those 30 days, then make the purchase. Obviously, this practice takes patience and discipline, and retailers are banking on your emotional response to a sale or advertisement. But financial decision-making is all about discipline, not emotion. The principle found in Proverbs 24:27 teaches us to "Finish your outdoor work and get your fields ready; after that, build your house." There is an order to our purchases and our monthly, livable budget helped to keep us on track.

Financial wisdom is discovering an order to things. You don't just one day decide to build a house. You dream, you develop a plan, and you save toward that building project. In other words, you do your homework for success and eventually you see the foundation to your home rising out of the dirt. In our own story, we had the land; but we still needed a house. Together, we prayed and sensed that the Lord would one day build us a house. But how that would happen was a mystery to us. At the time, I (Steve) was a social worker for a foster care agency. One of the foster parents I worked with was also very handy with a hammer and a saw. One day, he approached us and said, "I have six weeks of vacation saved up and if you're up for it, I'll help you build a house." We were blown away by this generous offer.

Over the next six months, he and I would literally build our home from the block basement up to a second floor. We hammered, we cut, we roofed, we drywalled, we pulled wires, and we glued pipes together. Eventually, we moved into our home with a bedroom for each child. It was a tremendous amount of work, but it was the house that God built on the land that God provided. He truly does all things well when we are willing to completely trust Him in all of our needs and our desires.

Needs vs. Wants

Another idea we incorporated was to establish two purchase lists—a need list and a wish list. The need list is an agreement to purchase as the funds become available, and the wish list is an agreement to purchase when we have extra, non-designated funds available. Ask yourself, "Do I/we really need this, or is it just something I/we want?" Another good question is, "Why do I/we need this, and do I/we need it right now?" It's amazing how many items one can purchase simply because they are on sale, which then accumulate and never get used— and why? Because they weren't truly needed.

Choosing Cash

Further, we made use of cash as often as possible, especially when we were in a retail environment such as a shopping mall. Studies indicate that we can spend up to 30 percent more money when using a credit card rather than using cash. There's something about the cash leaving our hands that provides more thought, more consideration. And while antiquated, writing a check has a similar effect; you have to physically deduct the amount in your checkbook, once again providing a second thought of, "Do I really need this?"

Properly Using Credit Cards

Another change to initiate is to use credit cards properly. By "properly," we mean pay each month's balance in full. Credit card companies are in the business of collecting interest when you allow the balance to roll over from month to month; don't give them that opportunity. If you cannot pay the complete balance in any given month or at the most two, stop using your credit card until you can pay off the balance. "Just as the rich rule the poor, so the borrower is servant to the lender" (Prov. 22:7 NLT). No matter from whom you borrow, you will become their servant until you've paid what you owe.

We received a notice from our credit card company in the mail about some policy changes. Opening up the envelope and reading some of the changes almost took our breath away. The new monthly interest on unpaid balances for our credit card was listed as 24.99 percent. It's easy to see how people can get caught up in the vicious cycle of credit card debt; don't let this happen to you.

Answer the following questions:

1. Do you currently use a budgeting tool? If not, can you commit to at least filling out the budget sheet in this chapter so that you can get a picture of your income and expenses?

2. What would be some of your financial goals? What do you want to accomplish with your money in the coming year, five years, ten years?

3. Do you currently carry a credit card balance from month to month? If so, do you know the interest amount you are paying monthly? Have you considered what this adds up to on an annual basis? Do you have a plan to reach a zero balance on your credit cards?

Emergency Savings Account

Rather than pulling out your credit card, we recommend building and maintaining a savings account of $2,000 to $3,000, at least. This way, when the refrigerator breaks or the car needs a new transmission, you can borrow from this account rather than using credit, and there will be no interest as you repay yourself over the following months. Be sure to pay the full amount back so that it will be available for future emergency needs. It is not that we should trust in those riches but that we are wise and think ahead to provide for any unexpected expenses. "Whoever trusts in his riches will fall, but the righteous will thrive like a green leaf" (Prov. 11:28).

Any savings beyond this level could be transferred into another account, such as a money market account where there are check-writing privileges. This secondary level of savings is a larger amount that you are saving for a larger purchase such as updating your vehicle or purchasing a home. Further, as it grows it can provide for you and your family in case of a long-term unemployment period.

Assets versus Liabilities

Assets are items we purchase whose worth will grow over time; by contrast, liabilities are items we purchase whose value depreciates as time passes. When you borrow money to purchase liabilities, such as a car, you can end up paying $15,000 for a vehicle whose price tag was only $10,000 five years earlier. This is because compound interest works against the value of the vehicle as it ages. On the other hand, when you take out a mortgage for a piece of real estate, you are actually making an investment in an asset that is increasing in value.

Many people live life never comprehending the difference between an asset and a liability. Borrowing money for something that decreases in value is a poor use of hard-earned income because it becomes of less worth the longer we own it. On the other hand, the longer you own your home, the more valuable it can become.

Proverbs wisely informs us to stay away from being security or surety for another. This is where you co-sign a loan to become the one responsible to pay if the party taking out the loan defaults. Unless you have a lot of cash sitting around, you and your spouse could actually lose your home in this process. "Do not be a man who strikes hands in pledge or puts up security for debts; if you lack the means to pay, your very bed will be snatched from under you" (Prov. 22:26-27; see also Prov. 11:15).

To save and to purchase assets rather than liabilities will create long-term wealth for you as a couple. Many people today live from paycheck to paycheck and then teach their children to do the same. Or, they live from loan to loan. When their children desire to purchase their first car, they introduce them to their banker so they can start their lifelong relationship with consumer debt, allowing others to earn money off of their purchases.

Consider the following:

1. Do you as a couple live in terms of assets or liabilities? Can you give any examples that back up your answer?

2. What ideas can you generate to create long-term wealth building?

3. If you are homeowners, do you have a plan to pay down your mortgage in order to retire the debt early? If you desire to become homeowners, are you saving to create a down payment?

More Ideas to Create Wealth

- Have a contest to see who can purchase a needed item at the best price.

- Share babysitting services with other families or take turns providing babysitting services to one another.

- Trade items for needed items. For example, you can trade labor so that you are installing a friend's tile while he is completing your electrical work.

- Have a yard sale to earn money from items you no longer use.

- Monitor websites such as eBay, Craigslist, and social networking sites for used items rather than purchasing them at full price.

- Use your public library for free books and films.

- Grow your own food or join a food co-op.

- Make wise use of coupons and in-store or online deals. Did you know that most food specials repeat themselves weekly or monthly? Ask the person behind the meat counter when your favorite items will go on sale. They will know the sale schedule.

- Schedule regular times to review your finances and financial goals. Some people call this a "money date." Do whatever it takes to remain on the same page financially. As a married couple, cooperate as a team, openly discuss every financial matter, and be accountable to each other.

- Figure out which of you is better at accounting and allow that person to take care of the monthly accounts.

- Normally in a marriage, one spouse is good at earning and the other person is good at controlling expenses. Share the responsibilities, agree as a team, and designate a leader. If you are not good at controlling expenses, then humble yourself and delegate the job or at the very least agree upon a spending limit. Also, agree on a spending limit for individual items that doesn't require consulting your spouse. And remember to limit the number of such purchases per month; they do add up.

Agreement is far more powerful than disagreement. When we agree ahead of time to the plan, then together we agree to the sacrifices that will need to be made. This level of agreement and communication can literally stop much of the fighting and arguing over finances.

As you live in moderation, exercise self-discipline, and are generous with others, you will soon discover more and more leftover money each month. Money and how we make use of it is an external indicator of who we are internally. Listen to these insightful words of Jesus: "Whoever can be trusted with very little can also be trusted with much, and whoever is dishonest with very little will also be dishonest with much. So if you have not been trustworthy in handling worldly wealth, who will trust you with true riches? And if you have not been trustworthy with someone else's property, who will give you property of your own?" (Luke 16:10-12). Our Lord actually indicated that how we handle our money will relate to how we handle His spiritual riches.

INTEGRITY TIES IT ALL TOGETHER

Lastly, Mary and I have found that integrity is the glue that holds financial decisions together. God desires to prosper us, but righteousness is His requirement. "Prosperity is the reward of the righteous." How does that happen? Because "the righteous hate what is false." Further, the Scripture reveals, "Righteousness guards the man of integrity" (Prov. 13:5-6,21). Dishonesty in any way, shape, or form will have a direct consequence in our finances. We dare not cheat the government or our employer and expect to prosper. Sometimes it takes humility to admit that we were wrong, made a mistake, or sinned, but the Lord honors humility: "Humility and the fear of the Lord bring wealth and honor and life" (Prov. 22:4).

True wealth goes far beyond money. In fact, it has nothing to do with money or riches. True wealth is not houses and land, silver or gold. Solomon discovered even among all of his possessions something far higher in value. He said, "By wisdom a house is built, and through understanding it is established; through knowledge its rooms are filled with rare and beautiful treasures" (Prov. 24:3-4).

Our home had four bedrooms and three of those four had our two sons and one daughter in them—truly our treasures. As a father and mother, we could not meet all of their wants, but we would give our lives to be assured that all of their needs were met. By far the biggest need they had was for a mother and a father to share with them the love of God and how He desired to be the One who could meet all of their needs—spiritual, material, and otherwise.

Their second biggest need was for their mother and father to love and respect each other as they loved each of their children unconditionally. We don't believe there is a child today who is better off with all the technology and toys they desire over loving, committed parents. No child cares about those things if their parents are divorcing. Security to every child today is not material items but the unconditional, unwavering love of a father and a mother.

For Mary and me, these principles have stood the test of time. God's Word has proven true time after time, and we have found that the very same God who owns the cattle on a thousand hills is the same God who desires to prosper you and your spouse. There is a warning, however—do not become legalistic in your financial decisions. Always allow grace to be your means toward others in financial decision-making. If you make an error, make the error on the side of blessing rather than withholding.

Answer the following questions:

1. How have you found integrity to be your "glue" when it comes to financial matters?

2. Take a few minutes to share with one another about some of your true treasures.

BUDGET SHEET INSTRUCTIONS

The following is a sample of the budget sheet that we first used to gain control of our financial picture. It helped us to quite literally see the full picture of our financial structure. We trust that it will do the same for you. Follow the directions as you record all of your annual income and then all of your annual expenses. While it can feel a bit overwhelming, the end result will be worth the time it takes.

Together, record the known or estimated monthly dollar figure for each category on the budget sheet. The definitions of the categories are listed below to help you determine the scope of each one. The completed example will serve as a guideline.

- Tithe: List your regular support (tithe) to your church. (Anything over 10 percent may be listed under the *Giving* category.)

- Tax: List all applicable taxes (for example, Federal, state, local, property, etc.).

- Investment: List any money invested for future care of your family (IRAs, retirement programs, savings accounts, etc.).

- Mortgage/Rent: List mortgage payment or rent payment.

- Maintenance: If you own your home, estimate monthly maintenance costs.

- Utilities: List your monthly utility costs—electricity, heat, water, sewer, trash.

- Telephone/Internet: Estimate your monthly phone bills, including cell phones, as well as cable and Internet costs.

- Food and Supplies: Include all homemade or packed meals, personal toiletries, and household products.

- Clothing: Estimate a monthly budget.

- Auto Payment/Lease: List auto payment(s) and the cost of insurance, driver's licenses, vehicle registration, gas, and maintenance.

- Medical/Dental: Include money spent for medicines and medical, dental, optical appointments.

- Gifts: List monthly expenses for gifts (birthdays, weddings, Christmas, graduations, etc.).

- Dining: List restaurant meals.

- Travel/Vacation: List weekend travel and yearly vacations.

- Recreation/Entertainment: List money spent for family activities and sporting events (swimming, bowling, movies, football games, etc.).

- Miscellaneous: List expenses not covered above—entertainment subscriptions, postage, magazine subscriptions, pet needs, artwork, music, etc.

- Personal Debt: List college loans, credit card bills, and any other loans.

- Giving: List charitable giving, ministry support, and special offerings or gifts.

- Savings: List money set aside for emergencies.

Indicate withdrawals with brackets. When the monthly budget amounts are completed, compute the totals. First, work from left to right, adding annual totals for each category. The annual totals added together, excluding income, can be more than, equal to, or less than the total annual income. Figure the average monthly total for each category by dividing each annual total by 12. If you discover a specific area of your budget sheet to be higher than you anticipated (for example, the miscellaneous category), try recording all of your expenditures in that category for one month. You may be surprised at the total when you keep record of every pack of gum or cup of coffee you purchase randomly.

Category	Jan	Feb	Mar	April	May	June	July	August	Sept	Oct	Nov	Dec	Amount Total	Average Total
Income: Husband	2250	2250	2812	2250	2250	2813	2250	2250	2812	2250	2250	2813	29250	2438
Wife	825	825	1031	825	825	1031	825	825	1031	825	825	1031	10725	894
Tithe	308	307	384	307	308	384	308	307	384	307	308	384	3996	333
Federal Tax	520	520	649	520	520	650	520	520	649	520	520	650	6758	563
State Tax	93	93	116	63	63	116	63	63	116	63	63	116	1208	100
County Tax	31	31	38	31	31	38	31	31	38	31	31	38	400	33
Investment / FICA	246	246	307	246	246	307	246	246	307	246	246	307	3196	267
Mortgage	0	0	0	0	0	0	0	0	0	0	0	0	0	0
Rent	550	550	550	550	550	550	550	550	550	550	550	550	6600	550
Maintenance	0	0	0	0	0	0	0	0	0	0	0	0	0	0
Electricity	95	95	95	95	95	95	95	95	95	95	95	95	1140	95
Heat	0	0	0	0	0	0	0	0	0	0	0	0	0	0
Water	0	0	0	0	0	0	0	0	0	0	0	0	0	0
Sewer	0	0	0	0	0	0	0	0	0	0	0	0	0	0
Trash	0	0	0	0	0	0	0	0	0	0	0	0	0	0
Telephone / Internet	100	100	100	100	100	100	100	100	100	100	100	100	1200	100
Food & Supplies	350	350	350	350	350	350	350	350	350	350	350	350	4200	350
Clothing	75	75	75	75	75	75	75	75	75	75	75	75	900	75
Auto Payment / Lease	0	0	0	0	0	0	0	0	0	0	0	0	0	0
Auto Gas	125	125	125	125	125	125	125	125	125	125	125	125	1500	125
Auto Insurance	0	0	750	0	0	0	0	0	750	0	0	0	1500	125
Auto License / Reg.	0	0	0	36	0	0	0	0	0	0	0	0	36	3
Auto Maintenance	75	75	75	75	75	75	75	75	75	75	75	75	900	75
Medical / Dental	80	80	80	80	80	80	80	80	80	80	80	80	960	80
Gifts	40	40	40	40	40	40	40	40	40	40	40	40	480	40
Dining	0	0	0	60	0	0	60	0	0	60	0	0	180	15
Travel / Vacation	0	0	0	0	0	0	300	400	0	0	0	0	700	58
Rec / Entertainment	30	30	30	30	30	30	30	30	30	30	30	30	360	30
Education	0	0	175	0	0	0	0	175	0	0	0	175	525	44
Subscriptions	0	36	0	0	0	0	0	0	0	0	0	0	36	3
Health / Life Insurance	50	50	50	50	50	50	50	50	50	50	50	50	600	50
Debt	0	0	0	0	0	0	0	0	0	0	0	0	0	0
Miscellaneous	125	125	125	125	125	125	125	125	125	125	125	125	1500	125
Giving	50	50	50	50	50	50	50	50	50	50	50	50	600	50
Savings	133	97	[321]	37	132	604	1228	1442	[1461]	73	132	429	500	42
Cumulative Savings	133	230	[91]	[54]	78	682	454	12	[1341]	[611]	71	500		

Personal Finances Budget Sheet

Category	Jan	Feb	Mar	April	May	June	July	August	Sept	Oct	Nov	Dec	Amount Total	Average Total
Income: Husband														
Wife														
Tithe														
Federal Tax														
State Tax														
County Tax														
Investment / FICA														
Mortgage														
Rent														
Maintenance														
Heat														
Electricity														
Water														
Sewer														
Trash														
Telephone / Internet														
Food & Supplies														
Clothing														
Auto Payment / Lease														
Auto Gas														
Auto Insurance														
Auto License / Reg.														
Auto Maintenance														
Medical / Dental														
Gifts														
Dining														
Travel / Vacation														
Rec / Entertainment														
Education														
Subscriptions														
Health / Life Insurance														
Debt														
Miscellaneous														
Giving														
Savings														
Cumulative Savings														

Chapter Nine

REBUILDING AFTER LOSS

*Love is a symbol of eternity. It wipes out
all sense of time, destroying all memory of
a beginning and all fear of an end.*
—AUTHOR UNKNOWN

*I am deeply aware of the disappointment and
hurt that my infidelity has caused to so many
people, most of all my wife and children.*
—TIGER WOODS

Mary and I were on a plane traveling to the Northwest and it was the dead of winter. We were conducting our first weekend marriage seminar in this frozen, sub-zero state. We jumped off the plane and onto the small airport tarmac to be greeted by the coldest wind we've ever felt. Our eyes began to water and our noses started to run.

As we became acquainted with the pastor of the church who met us at the airport, he informed us that we were going straight to the church building to meet with his two eldership couples who were awaiting our arrival. I thought, "Wow, he's not wasting any time putting us to work." He then said, "Am I glad you guys are here. We have a problem that we would like the two of you to address."

"What's the issue?" I asked.

He proceeded to say something we had never, ever heard before and haven't heard since. "It seems that the husband of our one eldership couple is having an affair with the wife of the other eldership couple," the pastor cautiously revealed. "We want you to meet with them." I then asked if the "non-affairing" spouses are aware of what had happened and was about to happen. He told us they were totally unaware of both.

I'm not sure who was more nervous and frightened about the meeting, the two of us or the couples we were about to meet. There we sat with the first couple, a bit stunned as the husband nervously confessed to his wife his ongoing affair. His eyes were constantly shifting to his spouse, then his pastor and then to us, but more often toward the ground. We watched as her face began multiple and visibly painful contortions. Her skin began to flush a bright red color starting from below her neckline and working its way to her forehead. And then the tears began to flow, nonstop. Her body slumped lower and lower in her chair. It was like she was literally shriveling up right there in front of us.

Humans seem to have the capacity to endure a lot of pain, both physical and emotional. We have all experienced traumatic, painful situations in our lives. How we choose to handle those hurts is important. We don't know why one person can maintain composure while another completely falls apart, but we are convinced it has something to do with how we interpret the event and then what we tell ourselves about the past, present, and most importantly the future.

It was in this meeting that we watched someone physically experience human pain—shortness of breath, heart palpitations, hands shaking in uncontrollable fear, and deep sighs that seemed to say, "What now?" Mary placed her hand on the wife's arm, but it was of little solace to her in a world that was literally crumbling around her.

164

A TRUE STORY OF PAIN AND HOPE

We sat down to interview Jon and Amy (names have been changed), a couple we have encountered who have a pain-filled story. With their permission, we are about to share with you their loss, brokenness, hope, and redemption.

Jon was sexually molested as a child. In his teen years, he succumbed to pornography and masturbation for comfort and intimacy. It was the beginning of a lifelong pattern of turning to pornography for the relief of pain, anxiety, and fear. He was addicted to the images on the screen. Eventually the addiction became more and more powerful in his life and he began to act out his fantasies. When he had extra cash available, Jon would visit a local prostitute, all the while hiding his dark and tortured secret life from his wife Amy.

One day, Amy received some pornographic pictures on her phone. She called the phone company and asked how that could happen if she never visited such websites. They told her someone most likely used her phone to access pornographic material. She questioned her sons, and then she questioned her husband. No one confessed. She prayed and asked God for wisdom.

She knew her husband had a "past issue" with pornography but had no idea of how current and active it presently was. She pressed in once again with Jon and he denied any involvement. "I felt so horrible," Jon said, "but lying seemed like my only alternative." He just couldn't believe he was at this point; he had been telling himself it would never get out of his control. That thought was now a past hope, not a present truth.

Meanwhile, Jon and Amy's 15-year-old son was diagnosed with medulloblastoma, a type of brain cancer. There were months of treatments, and Amy became the 24/7 caretaker of her son. Jon began to work longer hours and went deeper into his sin in an attempt to manage the emotional pain of having a very sick child.

I asked Jon why he lied to Amy about his sexual addictions, and he said, "To protect my sin." But then he went on to say, "Living in sin is going to bring pain, lots of it, but so is telling the truth. My denial kept me from change and being honest with myself, others, and Amy."

Jon spoke softly, "We have to decide which one is going to bring more freedom—lying or telling the truth. For a season, I thought that lying was the only way to keep pain from my wife and family. So, to be accepted and loved, I would tell others what they wanted to hear." This thinking kept Jon in denial, and his deep secrets kept him from change.

We turned to Amy. "As a wife, I discovered that I was married to a lie after it all came out. There is not a word in the English language that can explain what I felt when hearing about Jon's addiction and unfaithfulness."

Meanwhile, Jon wondered, *If she knows the truth about me, will she even like me?*

Amy continued, "Every foundation I stood on began to fall apart— my belonging, my acceptance, all within minutes of Jon's confession seemed to disappear," Amy shared. "My self-worth, my security, and my spiritual security just dissipated." Amy then said something we'll never forget hearing: "The sense of shame flooded me and I began to battle constant thoughts of, 'I'm not good enough,' 'I'm not pretty enough,' 'I'm just not enough,' and I ended up in a fetal position on our bathroom floor begging God to kill me."

After her confession, we asked Jon how he felt. "I had an immediate sense of relief and freedom in that I no longer carried the burden alone," he said. "The pain was even more severe because my wife was in pain and then I had to listen to her share her pain and not defend myself. Eventually," he revealed, "I had to take responsibility for the pain my wife was in, and in taking responsibility I realized that I was actually taking steps to become a man of integrity. Once I was finally dealing with the guilt and shame through being truthful, the guilt and shame actually began to decrease."

Questions to consider from this story:

1. Can you identify with any of the types of pain in this story?

2. What part do you feel pornography played in Jon's secret life of adultery?

3. In hindsight, when do you feel would have been the best time for this couple to talk about the secret life Jon was living?

4. Discuss how the lies we tell ourselves inhibit healing in our lives and in the lives of those we love.

5. Are there any secrets or struggles that you are keeping from your spouse? There is no better time than now to open up and talk about those struggles.

Jon and Amy were suffering from Jon's sin and from their son's cancer. Their son had a period of remission, but the cancer came back with a vengeance. Far too quickly, their son passed away, and now these two parents and their other children needed extra grace and healing from God, as well as the support from the friends and family who walked with them.

JON AND AMY'S STEPS OF HEALING

What follows is directly from the heart of this precious couple whose marriage has survived and is in the process of healing and becoming stronger again. These steps of healing are the redemptive part of their story, and they desire to share them with you.

1. Start making better choices through honesty and a spirit of humility.

2. Meet with your pastor/spiritual leader and tell your whole story. Leave nothing out and cover nothing up. Discuss present roles and responsibilities in your local church and evaluate any necessary changes.

3. Immediately start professional counseling.

4. Meet with any other spiritual leaders in your lives, share your story, and receive healthy input and discipline for your life.

5. The person struggling with sin needs a lot of intervention, counsel, prayer, accountability, and education concerning the sin and how it affects him or her as well as others.

6. The non-offending spouse needs just as much intervention, education in the truth, counsel, prayer, accountability, friendship, acceptance, and pastoral care.

7. Begin working toward forgiveness before working toward rebuilding trust. Forgiveness is key to healing.

8. Recognize that trust disappears through the fractured relationship. It must begin to be rebuilt, layer by layer. To rebuild trust, you have to start being honest in everything. There can be no more lies, not even one.

9. Be accountable and remain accountable to God, to one another, to your counselors and to your pastoral oversight.

FORGIVENESS IS A PROCESS

While we understand theologically that forgiveness is already granted from the cross of Jesus, for us as human beings who fall short of the glory of God it is a process. Jon and Amy stressed this to us over and over. Amy shared, "Forgiveness is an ongoing process, so are you working toward it or walking away from it?" This is a great question to ask ourselves in any situation that calls for extending forgiveness.

Amy told us that forgiveness called her to lay down her right to retaliate against her husband. "Even if it takes me five years," she said, "I need to keep moving forward in forgiveness regardless of whether my spouse finds personal freedom. I did and do find freedom in forgiving my husband. Without forgiveness, I would still be in my personal hell of tormenting thoughts."

Take a moment to review Jon and Amy's nine steps together, and ask yourselves if there are any areas where there may not be complete honesty and humility between you. Are there any lies you are holding on to? Are there any areas of denial that keep you from being totally honest with each other? If not, give God thanks. Express appreciation to your spouse for walking in faithfulness with you. If so, discuss how you can be accountable to one another in the area of marital faithfulness.

PORNOGRAPHY IN MARRIAGE

Pornography played a major role in Jon's downfall. For many, it is a silent killer. It's a killer of intimacy, of honesty, of time, of finances, and of our own bodies. Jesus said, "Your eye is the lamp of your body. When your eyes are good, your whole body also is full of light. But when they are bad, your body also is full of darkness" (Luke 11:34).

Our eyes provide a window to our mind, our heart, and our spirit. When our eyes wander toward or are attracted to pornographic images, we give darkness permission to enter the light. Jesus warned us about this very thing when He said, "See to it, then, that the light within you is not darkness" (Luke 11:35).

There is no redeeming factor when it comes to pornography. It is a multi-billion-dollar industry in our nation built on lust. Lust is insatiable, and Satan will hand it to us freely. Lust is about taking and is fully self-seeking. Lust will increase as we feed it until we find ourselves in bondage. But love is satisfying, focused on giving, and full of selflessness. As love increases, we will find ourselves walking in freedom and becoming closer to our life mate.

In our pre- and post-marital book, *Called Together*, we ask the question, "Can you be involved in lust toward your spouse?" That question creates quite a stir and challenges couples not yet married. A single person may think that marriage means the end of lusting after another, but married couples know that simply is not true. According to the above definition of lust, we can be involved in lust within our marriages by demanding, taking, and sexual selfishness. Pornography will feed that self-centered attitude.

Love feeds an attitude of giving, sharing, and bringing pleasure out of a heart and mind that is not tarnished by images of raw, base acts. Love is never demanding in the bedroom, as it speaks encouragement, affirmation, and genuine acceptance.

PORNOGRAPHY: THE BREAKDOWN WITHIN OUR MARRIAGES

A nationally conducted survey among churches over the past five years revealed that 68 percent of men and 50 percent of pastors view pornography regularly. The most shocking was that 11- to 17-year-old boys reported being the greatest users at 85 percent, and nearly 50 percent of young girls are also viewing porn (see fightthenewdrug. org).

Pornography is a $4 billion industry in our country. More money is spent on pornography per year than on professional baseball, basketball, football, and the Super Bowl combined. Eleven thousand adult films are produced per year, which is 20 times the number of regular media films annually coming out of Hollywood. The issue is sweeping through the church, reaching the next generation. It is an epidemic.

Studies show that when we are involved in sexual activity, the brain releases a number of chemicals, one of which is oxytocin, which is the "glue" that enables human bonding. (Oxytocin is also released as a mother holds and breastfeeds her newborn.) When we watch pornography, powerful neurotransmitters are activated. Our brain takes the images and associates this bonding chemical with them, actually interfering with natural human bonding and sexuality.

> *Therefore, prepare your minds for action; be self-controlled; set your hope fully on the grace to be given you when Jesus Christ is revealed. As obedient children, do not conform to the evil desires you had when you lived in ignorance. But just as he who called you is holy, so be holy in all you do* (1 Peter 1:13-15).

Viewing pornography opens the door of our soul and spirit to spiritual oppression, confusion, hopelessness, hurt, control, and domination in evil ways. Men and women feel betrayed by spouses who use porn. Women feel as though they cannot compete with the images their husbands are viewing. It is an illusion that says women will do anything to please their man; no woman in real life lives within that kind of fantasy world. It brings insecurities to her and can destroy her esteem. She will question her attractiveness and her adequacy as a lover. She can eventually think and believe that porn is more important to her husband than she is to him, an ultimate sexual betrayal.

Men often view pornography as innocent, a fix for loneliness or not having a sexual partner who agrees with his desires. Men rationalize and justify their behavior by attempting to call it "normal behavior" of a man who is simply visual. The act of viewing pornography is highly addictive and some psychologists state that it is similar to crack cocaine addiction. Over time it does not diminish, but tends to intensify. It can interfere in a man's ability to function at home with his family, at work, and, of course, in the bedroom.

Many women are now viewing porn. Six of ten girls see their first pornography before age eighteen. This practice has become far more acceptable among teen girls. For some, they are attempting to find out what boys desire, and for others they are involving themselves out of loneliness. Little do they know that viewing pornography creates an even higher rate of loneliness among its users.

Ladies and men, by viewing pornography you are supporting the industry and helping it to grow. You are contributing to the sexual exploitation of the victims caught in that world. You are adding to the sin of human trafficking. You are saying "yes" to an industry that feeds and preys on innocent men, women, and children and can even lead to their abduction, abuse, and death. You are learning to see and treat people as a sex object. You are destroying your marriage, your family, and yourself, and you are keeping victims trapped (which today includes more teenage girls and boys than ever).

Lastly, pornography will make you into a liar. You will have to constantly lie about your use to your loved ones and perhaps your employer. I love these verses that Paul writes under the inspiration of the Holy Spirit: "The body is not meant for sexual immorality, but for the Lord…. Flee from sexual immorality. All other sins a man commits are outside his body, but he who sins sexually sins against his own body" (1 Cor. 6:13,18).

Consider the following:

1. What has been your experience with pornography?

2. How are you dealing with it in your life right now?

3. How can you help one another remain pure and escape the pornography trap?

4. Do you have a same-sex friend who can help hold you accountable to not view pornography while you help hold him or her accountable?

We would like to encourage you to take an active stand against viewing pornography individually or as a couple. Consider making a commitment to have zero tolerance within your home for porn. Keep your computers within visible areas in your house and help hold one another accountable in this part of your lives. There is simply nothing redemptive about this behavior. It is also important to note that most children in their pre-teen years are introduced to pornography by their friends; consequently, it is vital to talk to your children about the dangers of viewing sexually explicit material.

For a list of resources, media, and websites, along with helpful material and information on sexual addiction, please see Appendix A.

Chapter Ten

STAYING TRUE

Will you love me in December as you do in May,
Will you love me in the good old-fashioned way?
When my hair has all turned gray,
Will you kiss me then and say,
That you love me in December as you do in May?
—JAMES J. WALKER

WHAT'S IN A VOW?

As wonderful as weddings are and as exquisite as they can look, they're not realistic. It has been said that the reason we take pictures at weddings is because it's most likely the last time we'll see anything that close to perfection. But no marriage is perfect, and reality does set in down the road.

On your wedding day, you spoke something called vows that probably sounded something like this: *For better or for worse; for richer or for poorer; in sickness and in health; 'til death do us part.* Rarely do we imagine having to face such issues. But truth be told, we will face some of these things and, perhaps, already have. If you think about it, these vows prepare us for reality long before reality sets in; they help prepare us for inevitable disappointments in marriage.

There is no perfect marriage because there is no perfect person in marriage. Author and speaker Jimmie Evens shares that if you think you found the perfect person to marry, you're mistaken. Not only is your spouse imperfect, you are imperfect as well. But here's the good news for those of us who are married and for those of us who desire to marry—marriage has a 100 percent chance of being absolutely fantastic, complete, and awe-inspiring if we commit to following our vows and biblical principles for marriage relationships. Just a short time into the marriage, we realize that we will need God to hold us together through our differences.

Mary is what I am not, and I am what Mary is not. But together, we make an amazing team.

Let's examine our vows:

1. What do you remember of the vows you spoke to each other in your wedding ceremony?

2. Are you actively walking them out, realizing the commitment you made to God, to one another, and to the ones who witnessed your vows?

3. When did you first realize just how different your spouse is from you? How did you work through that difference?

THE BROKENNESS OF AN AFFAIR

Exodus 34:14 says, "Do not worship any other god, for the Lord, whose name is Jealous, is a jealous God." We love the thought of jealousy that God has over us. God is jealous over you; it's a positive thing, righteous love. We also can become jealous as we bond with a life mate. To be jealous is to be intolerant of rivalry. Like God, we become jealous because we love. In God's jealousy, He protects—He guards His children from the foreign god, from idolatry. As husband

and wife we guard, we protect against a foreign intruder into our marriage. One of those foreign intruders is an affair.

An affair occurs when one person in a marriage takes the most sacred expressions of that marriage and gives them to another. Most people assume that there's only one type of affair—a physical, sexual encounter with someone who is not your spouse. But sex is not the only sacred expression of marriage, and you can have an affair without having sex. By giving away the emotional intimacy that should belong only to your spouse, you can have an emotional affair.

Today, emotional affairs are happening near, such as between coworkers, and far, oceans apart, through the Internet. Social media has become a huge source of marital failure as people rediscover "first loves" or feelings they once felt. In this way, you can have an affair and never meet the person face to face.

Dr. Gail Saltz, a psychiatrist at New York Presbyterian Hospital, said this concerning affairs: "Many people convince themselves so long as there is not sex, it is not an affair, but it is. It has to do with secrecy, deception and betrayal, and the emotional energy you are putting into the other person versus your partner. The most difficult thing to recover from is not sex, but the breaking of trust. Those involved in an emotional affair are often in denial. They do not think they're having an affair at all. The denial keeps them guilt-free, and they tell themselves, 'It's just a friendship.' But one in two emotional affairs becomes a full-blown, sexual affair."

Infidelity can affect all of our marriages because we can all be tempted. We are all potential vow-breakers. If we think it can't happen to us, we can become sloppy and less guarded, not alert to the enemy's schemes. To those of you who have given in to that temptation, this message is not to condemn you in any way. We serve a redemptive Savior, and He forgives.

How do you know you're in an emotional affair? Dr. Saltz shares ten clear warning signs:[1]

1. When your meetings are kept secret from your spouse

2. When you say and do things with someone you would never do in front of your spouse, or you would feel guilty if your spouse happened to show up

3. When you make it a point to arrange private time to talk with this person

4. When you share things with this person that you do not share with your partner

5. When you avoid telling your partner how much time you may be spending with this person

6. When you are stating things about your marriage that you should not be telling another, opening a window to your heart and unmet emotional needs

7. When you begin discussing your marital dissatisfactions

8. When you tell this person more about your day than you do your partner

9. When you "ready your appearance" in anticipation of seeing this person

10. When there is sexual attraction, spoken or unspoken, between you and this person

Even if there is no physical contact, these are signs of an emotional affair. The emotional high that the sexual attraction, the secrecy, and the euphoric feelings provide actually becomes addictive and will perpetuate the relationship.

To guard against ever having an emotional affair or to act in a precautionary manner, live your life the opposite of the above ten warning signs and institute clear boundaries. Setting boundaries around your marriage relationship is similar to a dating couple setting sexual boundaries. As a married couple, ask yourselves—what are we comfortable with and what are we not comfortable with concerning phone calls or driving in a car alone with someone of the opposite sex? What about lunch meetings with your opposite-sex boss? And how comfortable are we with a special opposite-sex friend who is, perhaps, married to another?

THE ANATOMY OF A REAL-LIFE EMOTIONAL AFFAIR

We had spent hours with Bethany and Greg (not their real names) in pre- and post-marital counseling. We knew them well. Now, married for five years, Bethany had a surprising confession. Here's the story in Bethany's words:

> Kevin was a regular customer of mine at the restaurant where I worked. He was abnormally quiet, so as a waitress I go out of my way to connect and help the quiet ones open up a bit. Over time, Kevin misread my approach; we became friends on social networking sites and began chatting quite often. Kevin was not a Christian, so I also saw it as an opportunity to share my faith with him.
>
> At the same time, my husband, Greg, began falling into somewhat of a depression from losses in life he was trying to deal with, silently, on his own. He stopped talking to me. He backed away from our relationship. So my conversations with Kevin actually helped fill a void. Eventually, Kevin became more comfortable sharing his feelings

with me, and suddenly I realized this "thing" was becoming inappropriate.

I decided to put some distance between us and attempted to "put Kevin in his place." Unfortunately, at the same time, I was lying to myself, because I actually craved the attention Kevin was providing. I found reasons to still be his friend, and we talked more and more online.

Realizing that I was thinking about him too much and returning affectionate hugs, I knew I had crossed a boundary and was in a full-blown emotional affair. There was no kissing, no private meetings, it was all in the restaurant or online. However, I was beginning to see how people in situations like mine begin to lose track of right and wrong. I would compare it to having a concussion—longing to fall asleep, all the while knowing that was the worst thing I could do. Meanwhile, my friends were in panic mode, with constant attempts to keep me "awake" in my marriage.

I was a wreck as I realized I had feelings for a man who was not my husband. Never in a million years would I have seen myself in this place. But something inside me said, "It's either this or a loveless, lonely marriage that's more like a prison." I found myself becoming more vulnerable. I knew it was a trap and yet, at the same time, I was falling for it.

But God and my friends were not letting me go. I couldn't shut out their voices. I began to realize that my husband was not just my soulmate because I loved him and was attracted to him; he was my soulmate because I chose him. I knew I needed to end my emotional connection with Kevin, but I made a huge mistake in doing so.

Boldly, I told Kevin I needed to end our relationship. I told him I was taking him off all my social networks, and I told him why—I was developing feelings for him. It was a huge mistake to say those words to that man. Kevin reacted not how I thought he would, but with even more abandon since he now knew I felt something toward him. Kevin was actually encouraged by my words, and the soul tie became stronger.

I set up roadblocks everywhere I could, but he was undeterred. Strangely, I was captivated by the fact that this man wanted me. I didn't know what to do; I wanted to run, but I also knew that it was going to take a lot of humility and hard work to make things right with my husband again.

I began to plead with God, "Please don't let me do this!" And of course God began working. One of my friends said to me, "Before you do anything, look long and hard into the future, because you will have consequences for these decisions. If you feel like you want to talk to Kevin, call me first and talk to a voice of reason." Then, Greg and I were invited to a yearlong marriage group to improve our marriage. Strangers approached me and spoke godly words over me. Many others believed in my marriage more than I did. I was so grateful for these voices of reason. I had asked, and my Redeemer kept trying to redeem. Healing came slowly. First, I had to grieve for what my relationship with Kevin could potentially become. Next, I did the Thirty Days of Encouragement for my husband, which also ended up changing me. And then I did the hardest part—I confessed to Greg.

I will never forget that hour. My dear husband, my soul-mate, looked at me and said, "This is my fault, not yours. I knew what you needed, and I didn't make an effort to meet those needs out of my own desperate needs. I know the evil one sent someone to you and you were vulnerable because of me."

But I knew I could not allow Greg to take all of the blame, and I told him so and asked his forgiveness for my emotional affair.

I asked Bethany what she would recommend for anyone who might find himself or herself in this very same place. This is what she said:

- Check your marriage foundation; ours was faulty.

- Realize that feelings are just that. Someone other than your spouse can stir up romantic feelings, and you can be vulnerable.

- There are different phases of love that marriages go through (some more difficult than others) as love matures.

- Keep a long-term perspective, and do not pursue a short-term gratification. When you look five or seven years down the road, you just might find yourself in the very same place.

- Keep making deposits into one another's love tank. When making deposits, you notice that person.

- If you find yourself thinking that you've fallen out of love, remind yourself that you can fall back in love in just the same way.

- Do something every day to build your marriage.

- Tell the truth. We each need the truth.

- Do regular date nights and take weekends away together. Keep building love.

- Keep dreaming together. Don't lose your dreams.

We think this is pretty good advice from someone who's been married for only five years.

Questions to consider:

1. What boundaries have you set in order to avoid an emotional affair?

2. What boundaries do you need to create for further protection?

3. How can you create a greater level of honesty and accountability with one another, especially when you find yourselves tempted to connect with someone outside of your marriage?

4. Share how the story of Bethany and Greg affects you and your marriage. What changes do you need to make in order to protect yourself and your spouse from an emotional affair?

5. How would you define an emotional affair?

6. Have you ever considered that an affair can be non-sexual? Why or why not?

What you can do as an individual if you've had an affair:

- Pray, confess it to God, and repent.

- Take responsibility. You allowed yourself into this situation, and you need to own it.

- Realize that you cannot remain friends with the person. Treat an emotional affair like any other affair, and cut all ties completely (stop calling, e-mailing, texting, etc.). If you do not thoroughly end the relationship, you will not rebuild trust with your spouse.

- Stop daydreaming about it. Turn your heart away from the affair and toward your marriage. Put your emotional energy into healing yourself and your marriage relationship.

- Hide nothing. Rebuild trust by being accountable with your whereabouts. As much as possible, go out only with your spouse, and be open about Internet and cell phone use so as not to allow questioning or wondering on his or her part.

- Look long and hard at why you had the affair and how you allowed yourself to be in that position. What were the underlying causes that helped drive you to seek attention or affection elsewhere (for example, difficulties in your marriage relationship, affairs in your family history, pornography, etc.)?

In addition to the above, here are steps you can take as a couple if one of you has had an affair or is tempted to have one:

- Move forward. Be totally honest and humble in all areas of life. Honesty severs all ties with the affair because affairs are built on lying and deception. Humility keeps you from becoming defensive and blaming another.

- Forgive one another. There is no greater response than the forgiveness of God through the love of His Son. He dwells within us so that we can extend that same unconditional love and forgiveness.

- Seek outside counsel and direction. Do not try to go it alone. Both parties, the offender and the offended, need godly wisdom and counsel as you work through a wide range of emotions.

- Reattach yourself to your spouse. Most likely you have moved away from one another in some areas of your relationship. Come together in prayer, dating, and fun; in reading God's Word; in finances and sex; in communication, mutual submission, servanthood, forgiveness, and godly counsel.

THE WHY, WHAT, AND HOW

If we will deeply and honestly consider the "why," "what," and "how" of an affair, it is our belief that we can more easily avoid such a disaster. Asking ourselves, "Why would I consider a relationship with someone who is not my spouse?" is a great place to begin. In other words, what is it in me that might be open to such a thought or action? Have I considered what it could look like down the road and what might happen as a result?

In answering these questions, we have to consider that we could possibly lose our life mate, our children, our job, our reputation, our ministry, our friends, and certainly our integrity. We may find ourselves in financial loss or ruin. We most certainly would suffer in our relationship with our Lord.

What is the purpose of committed love, and what will we do about it on a daily basis? When we consider what would have to take place for all of the aforementioned consequences, the level of destruction is frightening. If we lose the "why" of our marriage, we will most certainly also lose the "what" of our relationship.

Proverbs 4:23 says, "Guard your heart above all else, for it determines the course of your life" (NLT). When considering the "why," we must consider our heart, for it will determine the course of life we take. The heart is at the center of all we think and do, and the condition of our heart will allow for or guard both positive and negative emotions, thoughts, and words. We must intentionally guard our heart, or we will find the consequence to be unintentional actions.

Jesus clearly addressed this association when He said, "For from within, out of men's hearts, come evil thoughts, sexual immorality... [and] adultery" (Mark 7:21). Elsewhere the Scripture relates that Moses allowed certain consequences out of the hardness of men's hearts (see Matt. 19:8).

We have come to realize that when a person begins to lose their "why," it can almost always be detected that hardness within their heart has grown. The heart begins to close like a lily at the end of a long, sunny day. That closure will occur so slowly one might not even notice the heart change. If a spouse gives any portion of their heart, no matter how miniscule, to another, it is a portion that their spouse will not have.

We must maintain our heart toward intimacy with our Father and our spouse.

Philippians 4 encourages us toward what to think, keeping our minds occupied with truth. Earlier in that same chapter, we're admonished to not be anxious but to pray with thanksgiving, and the result will be peace, a peace that transcends all of our understanding, a peace that will "guard your hearts and your minds."

Ask yourselves:

1. How are we actively guarding our hearts?

2. Have we succumbed to hardness in any area of our hearts? In other words, through hurt, rejection, or in giving a portion of our heart away, have we allowed a seed of hardness to grow?

The "how" of an affair leads us into the schemes, secrecy, lying, and hiding. How do we go from being happily married to making time for another man or woman in an already busy life? How do we cover our tracks, and how do we lead two separate lives?

These might be a few of the obstacles to having an affair when we choose to look ahead and see the consequences. It's a scary thought that it could happen to us. It's vital to recognize our potential and even more vital to fight any temptation to move in this slippery and deceptive direction.

The psalmist David, who himself fell prey to such temptation, said this: "How can a young man keep his way pure? By living according to your word" (Ps. 119:9).

Finally, check out these verses of wisdom from King Solomon:

My son, pay attention to my wisdom; listen carefully to my wise counsel. Then you will show discernment, and your lips will express what you've learned. For the lips of an immoral woman [or man] are as sweet as honey, and her mouth is smoother than oil. But in the end she is as bitter as poison, as dangerous as a double-edged sword. Her feet go down to death; her steps lead straight to the grave. For she cares nothing about the path to life. She staggers down a crooked trail and doesn't realize it. So now, my sons, listen to me. Never stray from what I am about to say: stay away from her! Don't go near the door of her house! If you do, you will lose your honor and will lose to merciless people all you have achieved. Strangers will consume your wealth, and someone else will enjoy the fruit of your labor. ...Drink water from your own well— share your love only with your wife. ...May you always be captivated by her love. ...for the Lord sees clearly what a man does, examining every path he takes (Proverbs 5:1-10,15,19,21 NLT).

NOTE

1. Gail Saltz, M.D., *Anatomy of a Secret Life: The Psychology of Living a Lie* (Morgan Road Books 2006).

Chapter Eleven

GOING UNDER COVER(S)

I ran up the door, opened the stairs, said my pajamas
and put on my prayers—turned off my bed, tumbled
into my light, and all because he kissed me goodnight.
—AUTHOR UNKNOWN

Her kisses left something to be desired...the rest of her.
—AUTHOR UNKNOWN

We seemed to have reached a desperate part of our meeting with a middle-aged couple pastoring a small church in New York. In tears, the wife declared, "We're not intimate!" We asked what she meant by that statement. She said without hesitancy, "We don't do fun things together; we don't hold hands; we don't sit close any longer; we rarely have sex; and our conversations have become predictable, boring, and too infrequent. It's like we've taken a break from closeness, from our friendship...from intimacy."

Having heard her side of things, it seemed this couple had indeed lost intimacy. It didn't happen overnight and it wouldn't heal overnight, but there are ways to regain intimacy that we shared with them.

During the dating and engagement seasons, intimacy seems almost too easy. We are fooled into believing it will always be this way—easy and natural, without having to try very hard. But that's simply not true. After we say "I do," we sometimes stop pursuing or actively admiring our partner as we settle into a routine together. But it's crucial that we continue to desire and affirm one another and continue to pursue deeper and deeper intimacy.

How does a couple stay sexually active when there are jobs, a family, household responsibilities, and civic commitments, along with children's sports and school, and then local church involvement? All of these good things can rob us of intimacy as married couples and can even become priority over our sexual thoughts and desires. Sometimes life gets a hold of us, and all too often we're too exhausted to take a hold of one other.

We surveyed a number of couples as we prepared to write this book, and a large portion of those couples responded consistently in mentioning the need to maintain their sexual lives, their intimacy with one another. Most couples we have counseled over the years would express in one way or another that their intimacy desires are suffering, waning, or at the very least being put on the back burner for more pressing life priorities and pursuits. In our 40-plus years of marriage, we, ourselves, see that need.

THE GIFT OF INTIMACY

We were conversing with a missionary to China recently and he shared something astounding about the Chinese culture. He said there is a saying in this nation that affects their expression of marriage in huge ways. He first spoke the phrase in the Chinese language and then translated it for our understanding, "Marriage is the death of romance."

Truthfully, our God has been so gracious to us as human beings. In His creative act, He gave us a gift so precious, so intimate, and so intense that it seems reasonable to believe that the enemy of our souls would desire to steal it from us, fulfilling that Chinese saying. The animal kingdom only procreates, but mankind has the capacity to enjoy sexual intimacy outside of procreation. God gave us this gift within the committed boundary of a sacred relationship called marriage. Failing to continue to engage in sexual intimacy with each other is to turn your back on God's gift to you and to dishonor one another. Outside of physical or emotional limitations due to illness or abuses from our histories, we are to continue to give this gift of lovemaking to our spouse throughout our married lives.

Sex is about giving, serving, and meeting the needs of another. If it becomes about merely meeting our own needs, we have left God's design in order to pursue our own selfish desires. Any two people can be sexual, but sex outside of a committed marriage relationship becomes sex that is about "me" rather than about "us." It can quickly cross the line to love-taking rather than lovemaking.

A few questions about intimacy to consider:

1. How would you assess your sexual trajectory through your marriage so far? When was it really satisfying and why? When was it a challenge, and what incited those challenges?

2. How would you define intimacy within your marriage relationship? In other words, what does intimacy mean to you, and how does it relate to sex? How does intimacy not relate to sex for you? How does your mate define intimacy?

3. As a spouse, what are some ways you can continue to passionately pursue, affirm, and support your partner?

MARRIED SEX IS BETTER SEX

In a book by Linda Waite and Maggie Gallagher, *The Case for Marriage: Why Married People Are Happier, Healthier, and Better Off Financially,* the authors boldly state, "Married people have both more and better sex than singles do. They not only have sex more often, but they enjoy it more, both physically and emotionally." Here are some reasons behind their findings:

- **Proximity**—Sex is easier for married people; it fits better into everyday lives.

- **A long-term contract**—Married couples have more time to learn how to please their partners.

- **Exclusivity**—Married couples have more incentive to invest in their partners.

- **Emotional bonding**—In marriage, sex becomes a symbol of the partners' union, of their commitment to care for one another both in and out of the bedroom.[1]

We would add:

- **Safe sex**—Married sex is the only safe sex. Sexual encounters are dangerous encounters. While they may be full of excitement initially, they can cause worry and anxiety when they're with someone who is not wholly committed to you.

Author Kevin Leman once said, "If a couple spends just ten minutes describing their sex life to me, I'd have a pretty good handle on what's happening in the rest of their marriage." It's true; our sex lives can be a barometer of the whole of our marriage. So much of life is filled with mundane activities like changing diapers, driving to and from work, mowing the grass, and washing the dishes, but God has placed something truly extraordinary in our marriages through intimacy. He even dedicated a whole book of the Bible to intimate love—Song of Solomon. From a kiss, to a touch, to an "I love you" after the children are in bed, we can enjoy something that some have described as marital glue.

Picturing one of your intimate moments can allow you to realize that lovemaking provides the ability to connect not just physically but also emotionally and spiritually. This one act in marriage provides a window into one another's soul and builds on our ability to trust, to be fully received, known, and accepted just as we are. Like the first couple of the Bible who were described as "naked and not ashamed," we grasp the literal concept of oneness.

WE ALMOST LOST IT

Mary and I (Steve) were eight years into mission work, and we were living in a communal house. One evening, the phone rang, and a fellow staff member knocked on our bedroom door. We didn't hear him, so he then came into our room, interrupting an intimate moment. Mary froze in fear and embarrassment. Not only was our moment gone, but after that night Mary shut down sexually for several years. She struggled to become completely intimate in that house with the thought that someone might barge into our room at any moment.

We had children, and a similar issue occurred. Between the fear, busyness, and exhaustion, worry clouded her mind and directly affected her ability to respond sexually. Someone once said that for a man, sex erases problems but for a woman, problems erase sex. It was true for us.

I attempted everything I knew to do to love my wife emotionally. We talked, prayed, and worked on connecting in every room outside of the bedroom. I refused to push her or become angry with her, but at the same time I also knew that we were being robbed of God's gift to us. Finally, we agreed that we needed to enlist some help. We prayed and found some friends who were good at counseling couples with sexual issues. We discovered help, and fortunately we persevered through that difficult season of marriage.

Steve kept telling me (Mary) that God had more for us and there was a better, more intimate marriage available through sexual intimacy.

Sometimes I had faith to believe him and sometimes I didn't, but, eventually and with help, God gave us a strategy to not only recover but to experience romance afresh.

What about you?

1. Have you had any embarrassing encounters during intimacy that have created a blockage for one or both of you?

2. How is your sex life a picture of the whole of your marriage?

HOW WE GOT IT BACK

Sexual intimacy has a way of bringing to the surface what's happening in the lives of couples, and we were no different. You simply can't hide your emotions when it comes to giving yourself sexually. You can't fake not being shut down or not being angry or experiencing internal stress. But while sex exposes our hearts, it can also help bring healing to our lives.

As we chose the opposite of fear, self-doubt, and inhibition, life began to surface in this part of our marriage once again. But first, we did something radical, something we had never heard of before and perhaps something some would discourage couples from utilizing—an intimacy schedule. We agreed to frequency, the days of the week, and the approximate time, and we wouldn't allow anything to deter us from our schedule. But how did something so seemingly rote as a schedule bring healing to our intimacy issues?

First, it helped to prepare us mentally. Second, we knew that it wasn't an option; we were committed. Third, it brought freedom—for Mary in that she knew what to expect and when to expect it, and for me in that I knew I wasn't going to have to ask for intimacy and hear yet another "no."

A schedule can actually increase sexual desire. It engages the brain and the brain engages the rest of our body in preparation. It provides a reminder to begin to think about connecting physically. For me (Mary), it offered the chance to think about and prepare my mind and body for lovemaking. I could incorporate thoughts of receiving Steve's advances without the fear of interruption and embarrassment.

A schedule can also show value and grow anticipation. What we value in life, we will place on our schedules. We schedule most everything in life that is important to us; is this any less important? When we have something scheduled to look forward to, we anticipate it. I (Steve) love anticipation. Whether it's celebrating Christmas, going on vacation, or hosting visitors, I love the anticipation that precedes these events.

Finally, when we honor our word by keeping a schedule, we build trust as a couple. And when we build trust, we deepen our relationship.

Is your marriage in need of a schedule? Answer the following questions to find out:

1. Would it help our sexual relationship to begin an agreed-upon schedule for intimacy?

2. If so, what would be our agreed-upon frequency and day(s) of the week?

3. What is our preferred time of day?

4. How can we be held accountable to stick to our commitment?

Many will say that scheduling sex reduces spontaneity, but we counter that thought with this: scheduled sex is better than no sex. And truly, as we stick to our schedule, we will eventually realize an increased desire and, perhaps, find ourselves breaking the rules by being intimate spontaneously.

THE NUMBER ONE INHIBITOR

The benefits of a healthy sex life far outweigh any inconvenience in time. The most frequent excuse we hear from couples is that life is just too busy and most are overcommitted with responsibilities. We are told that the average couple doubles their responsibilities every ten years of marriage. We're running everywhere but into one another's arms. Most of us are so tired from giving 100 percent all day that we fall into bed exhausted, night after night, with nothing left for each other.

When we give ourselves to everything else in life but do not prioritize one another enough to honor our vows in our own bedrooms, our marriages suffer. Your marriage came before your children, and it will need to be intact once your children are raised and leave home. If you have nothing left for the closest person in your life, then you are directly dishonoring the gift so graciously given to you by your Creator.

A CLEAR BIBLICAL PRINCIPLE

There is a very clear principle found in the book of First Corinthians. These scriptures are so important when it comes to intimacy within marriage that we want you to read and visualize them:

> *The husband should fulfill his marital duty to his wife, and likewise the wife to her husband. The wife's body does not belong to her alone but also to her husband. In the same way, the husband's body does not belong to him alone but also to his wife. Do not deprive each other except by mutual consent and for a time, so that you may devote yourselves to prayer. Then come together again so that Satan will not tempt you because of your lack of self-control* (1 Corinthians 7:3-5).

After reading this scriptural reference, discuss the following questions:

1. When the writer, Paul, speaks of "marital duty," he is speaking of intimacy as husband and wife. How are you as a couple doing with your "fulfilling"?

2. To whom does your body belong? Yes, it is God's, and yes, it is yours to care for, but what does it mean when we are told that our body is not just ours but our spouse's?

3. Have you ever "deprived" one another? If you have deprived each other, what are the reasons or excuses you used? Have you ever deprived one another so that you could concentrate on your prayer lives?

4. The writer indicates that to not be sexual is to open ourselves to immorality, or at least the temptation. Have you viewed your sexual lives as that important? Why or why not?

5. Have you taken notice of the gravity of what these scriptures are actually saying to married couples? Can you refuse to be sexual, deny one another the gift given by God, and then not be held accountable to Him for your actions?

While we realize there are many extenuating circumstances, and we are certainly not interested in heaping condemnation on anyone, we want to recognize that couples are giving up and giving in to something that is less than best for their marriage.

WHOSE BODY IS IT, ANYWAY?

When our sex lives become stagnant, so many other parts of our relationship can also become stagnant. We can allow the little things to pile up and bother us; we can become frustrated and short with each other. When there is little or no sexual release, anger gets much closer to the surface. We can also find ourselves not connecting as often through nonsexual touch. Ultimately, we discover that our emotional and spiritual connections become fraught with difficulty.

When we decide that our body is not our own but our life mate's, we cross a river to find that the other side is even more pleasurable. Sex outside of marriage can never provide anything this close, this intimate, or this loving. We can have eyes, hearts, and passion for each other only. Our life under the covers will become exciting again, fulfilling and pleasurable as we discover one another anew.

If you have taken a break from intimacy, pray and come together again so that neither of you is tempted by the evil one. We find it interesting that prayer is cited in connection with our married sex lives. Perhaps in God's creative design, the two were always to be considered working together toward our physical, emotional, and spiritual unity.

WHEN SEX BECOMES UNHEALTHY

Let us share with you some areas that we find unhealthy when it comes to a sexual relationship. We have heard these over the years and have maintained a list of unhealthy patterns of sexuality within marriage relationships.

- Sex should never be used in a physically or emotionally abusive way.
- Unhealthy sex will cause another to feel devalued. We should never desire to devalue our spouse.
- When sex is purely for self-gratification, it is self-centered, and self-centered sex is unhealthy.
- Neither partner should ever feel shame from sexual activity. If shame is a result, you should reevaluate what you are requesting of one another.
- Neither partner should feel forced to be involved in a sexual activity against his or her will.

- When love is not at the core or the center of sexual intimacy, it is unhealthy.

- It is unhealthy to withhold sex as a form of punishment or anger.

- Sex should not be used or take the place of affection, touch, or closeness.

- We should never defile our marriage bed by engaging in sex with anyone other than our marriage partner.

WHAT INHIBITS INTIMACY?

- Overscheduling, self-depletion, fatigue

- Lack of communication

- Selfishness, not serving one another

- Lack of non-sexual touch

- Pornography (false intimacy)

- Not planning times for intimacy

- Poor hygiene

- Unresolved conflict

- Lack of prayer, spiritual connection

- Control issues or lack of mutual agreement

- Attraction issues

- Lack of respect (emotional connection)

- Lack of affirmation (verbal connection)

PRACTICAL INTIMACY BUILDERS

1. Pray together regularly.

2. Share the workload in and out of the house.

3. Go on date nights to spend quality and quantity time together.

4. Hold family nights and interact with your children together.

5. Take weekends away or overnights at least once every few months.

6. Evaluate your relationship. (See Chapter 12.)

7. Read books and listen to messages on intimacy.

8. Seek counseling help and input before your issue becomes severe.

9. Schedule sex.

10. Spend time connecting through daily conversation.

PHYSIOLOGICAL AND EMOTIONAL BENEFITS OF A HEALTHY SEX LIFE

1. Sex has major physiological benefits. As exercise, it creates an increase in your heart rate, which burns calories.

2. There is an increase in blood flow, which provides an increase in endorphins, natural pain-relieving and pleasure-inducing chemicals. As a natural analgesic, sex is a great pain reliever.

3. Sex is a great sleeping pill. Perhaps you are worried or anxious about something and find it difficult to quiet your mind. An orgasm can help bring you to a state of natural relaxation, helping you to fall asleep.

4. Sex can help to relieve pre- and post-menstrual symptoms, as it increases blood to flow to the pelvic region of the body.

5. Sexual intimacy creates positive emotions and brings a sense of contentment.

Sexual intimacy is something we grow in, but even more so, something that grows in us. We share this act of marriage with the love of our life. Keep making it a priority and build upon what you have today for even better lovemaking in the future. Refuse to allow intimacy to be stolen from you. God so loves you that He gave you this extraordinary gift. Pray about your sex life. Cherish it, all the while protecting it.

NOTE

1. Linda J. Waite and Maggie Gallagher, *The Case for Marriage: Why Married People Are Happier, Healthier, and Better Off Financially* (New York: Doubleday, 2000).

Chapter Twelve

INTIMATE CONVERSATIONS

True love stories never have endings.
—RICHARD BACH

*Do I love you because you're beautiful, or
are you beautiful because I love you?*
—RICHARD ROGERS and OSCAR HAMMERSTEIN II, *Cinderella*

Before you were married, did anyone advise you that your marriage would need room for failure, forgiveness, loss, brokenness, disagreement, or even sin? If not, a full and honest disclosure was missed, and you may have entered into marriage a bit naïve or ill-advised. Marriages fail because we fail God, each other, and ourselves. We fail to love, we fail to honor, we fail to forgive, and we fail in keeping at bay our own personal struggles with selfishness.

Perhaps that all sounds a bit too negative, but at the same time we need to deal with the reality of our own lives here on earth. God created us for a Genesis 1 and 2 world, a perfect world, but we presently live in a Genesis 3 world, a fallen world. That fact in and of itself can provide a lot of awareness to why marriages fail. It can also provide insight into how we can avoid failure.

203

You obviously desire to not have your marriage fail, or you wouldn't have made it this far in this book. We applaud you whole-heartedly for that.

The Genesis account states that God created us for a world where mankind was first introduced to God's idea called marriage, and within that world this same couple personally walked with God on a daily basis. Can you imagine as a couple that at the end of each work-day, after dinner, you would take a stroll in God's perfect garden and speak with Him as you would any other person? How that must have refreshed them, reenergized them, and built them for life together, for family, and for their next day working in that same garden.

But can't God walk with us on a daily basis today? Can we not have a conversation with Him together about our marriage, family, business, or life questions? Would we be amiss to entertain for one moment that God has stopped caring for those He created to bear His image after Genesis 3? It is this discussion that takes us to the most intimate act of marriage—prayer.

Take a moment to discuss your individual prayer lives:

1. When do you pray and about what life concerns do you pray?

2. Are the two of you connecting in prayer? If so, do you find that connection comfortable, or do you feel as though you need to grow in that prayer con-nection? What areas of growth do you perceive are needed?

3. If you do not feel as though you are connecting in prayer, why not?

TALKING TO GOD TOGETHER

You can be sexually intimate with almost anyone, but you can-not pray with just anyone. In order to really open up our hearts and pray together, we must know we are in a safe place. We must know we are not being judged for our heartfelt prayer. And we must know that the one to whom we divulge our heart will maintain confidentiality and that we can trust them with our deepest, most secret sins and needs. Praying together within marriage is so intimate that if these factors are not present, we will almost always divert ourselves to a same-sex prayer partner for that level of prayer. At the same time, we will be forfeiting something so intimate, so close and so heartfelt, that a certain dimension will be missing within our marriage relationship.

If I (Steve) would spend a few months praying with your husband or if I (Mary) would spend a few months praying with your wife, we would know them better than most people on the earth today, even those closest relationships. Why?

Let's say we meet together every Monday morning from 6:00 to 6:30 and all we do is pray. No conversation, no coffee, and no news or sports updates—just prayer. In time, as trust builds, we will begin to reveal our hearts, our deepest issues in life, and our deepest needs and longings. Our inner lives will be exposed, and we will go beyond words, beyond life issues, right to the heart. As we hear each other's hearts, we will reach an intimate place.

So many couples avoid or miss that level of intimacy by not connecting in prayer together. Mary and I often prayed when we were first married. We prayed at the meal table and at night as we closed our day. Sometimes we prayed in the car together while traveling. But when we got desperate for our children while they attended school or experienced life's complications, we realized a need to go deeper and to connect daily in prayer for these needs.

Also as a mom, I (Mary) realized that I could worry and fret, or I could pray with my husband and trust my heavenly Father for my children's needs. As parents, we realized early on that we could not meet all of our children's needs, but we had faith in the One who could. The more we prayed, the more we wanted to pray, and the more we wanted to pray, the more answers to prayer we discovered.

One day our son Marc came to me and said, "Mom, someone stole several of my really expensive books out of my locker, I don't know what I'm going to do to replace them." I told Marc we would pray and ask God to return those books. While he looked at me with a funny, questioning expression, we both knew those books were gone forever unless God intervened.

Steve and I, along with our son, committed to pray daily for the return of his books. At the end of the week, Marc returned from school and announced, "Guess what? My books showed up in my locker today...out of nowhere!" We knew Who went to work on the issue for us, for our son, and we gave Him the credit. It was a huge prayer life lesson for us as a family, and one that our son was able to identify as the personal hand of God in his life.

Can we challenge you as a couple one more time, in hopes of provoking you to establish a regular and intimate prayer routine? We must incorporate our relationship with God through prayer in order to ask of Him, rather than requiring all the answers from our spouse. We need the intervention of our Lord simply because we will all too often come to the end of ourselves.

Start small; find five or ten minutes in your day to connect in prayer. Begin your prayer time by giving God thanks for all of His blessings in your life, including each other. Move on to praying for one another and then your family, along with any other needs. Close again with prayers of thanksgiving, because a thankful heart is an encouraged and an encouraging heart. As this time of prayer becomes a habit, allow it to grow and increase. The Bible says that when we find a place of prayer, we find a place of power and agreement (see Matt. 18:19-20).

Some questions to consider:

    1. How and when can you initiate praying together?

2. When is the best time of the day to connect in order to give thanks and requests to God?

3. If you already experience the intimacy of prayer, how can you see your prayer lives grow?

4. What are some of the areas that you can begin to pray about that you have not yet addressed?

GROWING OUR FRIENDSHIP

One of the ways to grow your friendship as a couple is to connect spiritually in prayer. We have discovered that when we connect in prayer, we also communicate. Mary and I have given each other permission to interrupt our prayer time in order to communicate a detail perhaps forgotten in conversation or to ask a question. This practice has furthered our emotional connection with each other.

Over many years of marriage, we can honestly say that we have become best friends. How has that happened, and what does that practically look like?

Friends are attached to each other through feelings of affection or personal regard as indicated by the dictionary. But a marriage friendship is far deeper than that and far more meaningful. Marriage friendship must go deeper than feelings of affection to emotional, physical, spiritual, and financial closeness.

We are best friends because:

- We talk about everything.
- We share the deep things that we share with no other human beings.
- We are confidential about our relationship and what we share.
- We never lie to each other about anything. (Well, except one year, when Steve was planning a surprise

party for me, and some of his conversations seemed somewhat…evasive!)

- We trust one another entirely.
- We feel safe with each other in every way—physically, emotionally, spiritually, and financially.
- We anticipate events and make plans together, such as the birth of our children and grandchildren, travel, retirement years, etc.
- We are fully open and vulnerable with each other.
- We are always there for one another in the good and the not-so-good times.
- We do not walk away from each other or give each other the silent treatment.
- We cheer one another on.
- We celebrate each other's successes.
- We never make fun of one another or belittle the other.
- We never participate in family or group discussions that are not uplifting of the other.
- We stand by one another, especially in times of failure.
- We serve one another.
- We anticipate what the other might need and do our best to provide it.
- We are proud of one another and never jealous of each other.
- We exercise together.
- We minister and complete our co-mission together.
- We work on our yard and in our kitchen together.

- We laugh a lot.

- We go on dates and weekends away, just the two of us.

- We truly listen to one another and work hard at not interrupting.

- We pray together about every area of our lives.

- We still kiss; we still hold hands; we still say, "I love you" several times a day.

Friendship is a part of our growing intimacy. It can be a vital part of yours too. Consider the following questions before going further in this chapter:

1. Looking back over this list, what would you add that has helped to create and strengthen your friendship?

2. What are you already doing or what can you incorporate from this list to build an even deeper friendship?

HEALTHY RELATIONSHIPS REQUIRE REGULAR EVALUATION

Do you experience evaluations at your work place? Evaluations have gotten a bad rap due to their connection with raises or the lack thereof. We, however, have come to believe that an evaluation can be a healthy, positive, necessary, and intimate thing to do within our marriages. Anything of worth or value to us is also worth evaluating.

I (Steve) regularly took my children on "dates" as they were growing up. We would go out to a restaurant, and I would ask them questions like, "How am I doing as your dad?" "How am I doing as your mom's husband?" "Have I been away too much or given ministry too high of a priority?" Those were questions of evaluation by nature. I wanted to hear from my children about how they felt I was doing. They had feelings that needed to be heard. I wanted them to know they were valued enough that I wanted to hear their opinion and feedback.

I can remember when our daughter, Brooke, was anticipating her very first date with her dad. She knew her brothers had that privilege, but up to that point she had not. We went to breakfast at a local restaurant and I began to ask her my frequently used line of questions that I had used with her brothers. Meanwhile, Brooke was playing with her silverware, at times under the table, and at other times standing on the vinyl booth seat. I didn't get many questions in until she stopped, looked at me and said, "Daddy, these questions are stupid!" Right, perhaps age four was a little young to provide critical analysis to her father.

I have done the same with Mary. I love her honest and insightful feedback to me. Her truth has helped me to grow as a husband, a dad, a minister, a friend, and a man. Why would I not ask her questions of evaluation when she is the one who observes my life more closely than anyone else on the earth?

After I speak a message or complete a training, it's her opinion that I value most. She will not patronize me or appease me, but what she will do is tell me the truth. I might ask something like, "Tell me two things I did well and one or two things I could improve upon." She will be loving and grace filled, but she will be honest, and it's the honesty I'm looking for.

How about you? Can you handle honest input into your life from your spouse or your children? Could you ask the question, "Tell me two things I do well and one or two things I could improve upon?" Can you think of questions of evaluation that you have asked of each other?

TAKING YOUR MARRIAGE ON AN ANNUAL EVALUATION RETREAT

We have a practice of ending each year by taking an overnight trip to a nearby hotel for the purpose of evaluating the past year and praying about vision for the next. We want to share this practice with you so you might also benefit from this extremely intimate and valuable process.

Mary and I highly anticipate this time every year because we feel as though we connect in the spiritual realm, the emotional realm, and in the practical, stuff-of-life realm. We leave this getaway with a greater sense of oneness, direction, and purpose.

We always begin our retreat with an extensive time of giving thanks to God for all He has done in the past year, all of His provision, and all of His faithful direction. After giving thanks we move to evaluating our financial year. We take our budget sheet, checking and savings account information, retirement accounts, mortgage balance, tithes and giving, and anything else that has to do with our household finances, income, and expenses. We discuss it all and make decisions like paying extra on the mortgage in order to retire the debt early or discerning if any budgeted item is experiencing a shortfall.

One year, we knew we had to decrease our overall budget by 7.5 percent due to a decrease in Steve's salary. I (Mary) was dreading this time because finances were what we normally had disagreements about. But first we prayed, and then we started cutting, and we came up with a very livable budget less 7.5 percent. This mutual agreement took us into the next year with faith for our needs to be met.

During your evaluation, review all of your bank accounts. Review your giving (tithe, missions, firstfruits, and offerings). Review your investments, such as life insurance, money market savings, and retirement funds. Review your debt and your plan to get out of debt. Are you in agreement with your spending, credit card charges, and investments? Are you putting enough away for emergencies and retirement? Are you meeting your financial goals in all the above areas?

What are your future financial goals? What are you saving toward? How are you handling your children's higher education? When will you next update your vehicle? What maintenance and improvement projects do you need to consider around the house?

The overall question we're asking every year is, "What is our financial plan?" Many couples do not use a budget or develop a short-term or long-term financial plan. It is an extremely helpful way to be in agreement and to reach those financial goals.

Why else should we do all this? Proverbs 3:9 tells us to honor the Lord with our wealth. We truly believe that when you operate in financial agreement, you will experience God's blessing.

We move on from financial evaluation to reviewing our employment, side business, not-for-profit boards and volunteer activities, children's activities, and what school they will attend in the coming year. Everything is on the table, and we do mean everything. If you are teaching Sunday school this term, does that mean you are to teach it next term? If you are taking college courses, are you to continue them? Are you planning a family mission trip? Is this the year to realize that trip?

Never assume that what you are involved in this year will happen forever or even the following year. Mary was the head of a local campaign for many years. It consumed a lot of her time because she oversaw the entire campaign, including all the volunteers and their various activities. One year I asked her, "Are you supposed to continue with your annual campaign?"

She asked, "What do you mean?" I didn't think we should presume that what we have done for years is what we are to continue do in the coming year or years. It's easy for us to go on autopilot and keep doing the same things while constantly committing to new activities. That's why we were evaluating—to avoid those ruts and overextensions. We discovered that we might be saying "Yes" to something that keeps another person, perhaps the right person at the right time, from having the opportunity to lead.

We prayed, and Mary sensed that she was to lay down the campaign once she had identified and trained a new leader to take her place. Evaluation provided that little bit of change and, at the same time, provided us with a greater sense of agreement.

Next, focus on your schedules. Review your activity level from the past year. Were you gone from home too often with employment or hobbies? Did you enjoy a sufficient number of dates with each other and your children? Did you have weekends away? Did your family take a vacation? Assess your children's activities and their schedules. Share your anticipated schedules for the coming year. Project time away together and family vacation. Project this evaluation time for next year.

Another activity that we engage in as a part of our vision-seeking is to ask our heavenly Father what scriptures He might be speaking to us for the coming year. We have always found this exercise to be encouraging and uplifting. Further, we record these scriptures, along with our goals and co-mission statement, all in a single document so that it's easy to reference over the next 12 months and easy to review the next year.

The next step is to review any written or verbalized goals from that previous year. Review your marriage mission statement and make any necessary changes. Review any scriptures that you had recorded from the past year. Write your new goals and vision (spiritual, financial, social, emotional, mental, and physical). Finally, wrap up your time away by dreaming ahead. Pray and record what you see, and allow your mate the freedom to project into the future because "faith is being sure of what we hope for" (Heb. 11:1).

One year, Mary and I left our annual evaluation and vision time with 12 goals to complete or to believe for completion in the following year. When we returned to our evaluation weekend that next year, we discovered we had only completed three of the twelve. We laughed as we realized that our goals needed to become more realistic, practical, and fewer, but at the same time, faith-filled for the future.

SOME QUESTIONS ABOUT EVALUATION

1. Have you taken the time to ask questions of each other that were in the form of evaluation?

2. When can you prioritize your first evaluation get-away?

3. What pieces of the evaluation process as described above will you each be responsible for?

4. How do you each perceive evaluation helping to grow your intimacy?

For an abbreviated evaluation template, see Appendix B.

Increasing intimacy within your marriage advances through prayer, growing your friendship, and evaluation. This process, as long as it is both grace-filled and truth-filled, will enhance your *staying together* day by day and year by year. The bond of intimacy will keep you strong in your commitment as your love grows deeper.

Chapter Thirteen

THE SIX MOST
IMPORTANT WORDS

For you see, each day I love you more. Today
more than yesterday and less than tomorrow.
—ROSEMONDE GERARD

You can give without loving, but you
can never love without giving.
—AUTHOR UNKNOWN

We have to ask, because this is the last chapter: Did you get married thinking about what you were giving up or did you get married thinking about what you were going to gain?

I (Steve) tell everyone that I married up and I truly did. I received a gift from God that was beyond my dreams in my wife, Mary. She has been a joy to become one with. Yes, we have disagreed and yes, we have had differences, but isn't that love? I would not fight with the person whom I do not know on the street. I have nothing invested in that relationship, but I have everything, my all, invested in my marriage.

And I (Mary) felt incredibly blessed to be marrying a man who was passionate about his relationship with Jesus. Most of the "Christian" guys I knew were at church and youth group because their parents required them to attend. In Steve's love for the Lord, he was excited to be learning and growing in his faith and that excited me. He was a young believer but had a maturing and deepening spiritual walk. I wanted to share the rest of my life with this man and knew that I was gaining someone who would lovingly lead me and value me because he so valued God.

We are settled. We do not have to always agree, but rarely do we disagree. Steve is Mary and Mary is Steve and we desire the very best and the highest goodwill for each other. We are not competing with one another and we are not jealous of each other. We will not settle for mediocre in our relationship and we will not allow a spirit of discontentment to show its ugly head. We both know that through the grace of God and His goodness to us, we gained something...or someone in marriage. When we said "yes" to one another, we said "no" to every other possible partner out there. We have no regrets.

GROWING YOUR MARRIAGE INTO DECADES

How did we make it over the 40-year mark in marriage? First, we must walk in a truth that says what we experience today is a direct result of how well we walked out our marriage yesterday. We believed in the biblical principle that says what we sow, we will reap (see Job 4:8; Gal. 6:7-8). What seeds we sowed in our 20s, 30s, 40s, and 50s are what we reap today in our marriage. Those seeds directly reflect and affect where we are in our marriage at this point in time. Do not let anyone tell you otherwise. Sow good seeds every day of your marriage!

Do not procrastinate. Procrastination will slowly kill a relationship. The longer we take to fulfill our word, the more irritated our spouse can become. Taking care of issues as soon as you can will benefit you long term. At the same time, allow your spouse some space to prepare for dealing with an issue. Do not follow him or her around the house pushing for resolve when one of you is not ready.

Make your marriage of higher priority than the issues you are dealing with. Your marriage was before the issue and it will be after. Realize that you must practice in the dark what you learned in the light. Issues will come and go, so even in disagreement do not make the issue more important than the health of your marriage. Mary and I, even in disagreement, always strive for alignment.

Never stop investing in one another and in yourself. First, if you are not taking care of yourself, then you are not taking care of the one you are married to. If you do not care about you, you are saying that you do not care about your life mate.

Pursue personal growth. The healthier you become, the healthier your marriage will become. The closer to God you are, the closer you will be with your spouse. There is a direct correlation between these two and this principle is true even if you are not a Christian believer.

There will always be seasons of marriage that are dull, boring, and gasping for air. That's life. We will not always feel the feeling that we felt when we first met and were dating. Life is boring sometimes, but we persevere through those times in order to reach the fresh and new life encounters that will come.

Recently, I (Steve) was asking my three-year-old grandson if he would like to attend a rather long sporting event with his grandparents. He looked at me as if to say yes, but before answering me, I added a question. I asked him if he would find that event too boring. With a smile he said, "Papaw, that would be too boring." Not knowing if he knew what the word boring meant, I inquired. He replied, "Boring means it would hurt my stomach." He was right. Boring does hurt your stomach sometimes, but admit that you are at a boring stage of life and marriage, and in confessing it you can then begin to take steps to remedy the staleness.

Find something beyond yourselves. Serve something bigger than your marriage, your family, and your jobs. Engage in a marriage conference and keep learning. Read books to improve who you are as a person. Grow in your leadership skills. Head downtown and serve the homeless in your community. Take a risk and go outside your normal routine. Go on a national or international mission trip.

When our children were young, ages 8, 13, and 15, we flew as a family to a mission school in the nation of Guatemala. We stayed in a not so nice mission house, ate rice and beans all week, taught English classes, painted school rooms with paint that was no thicker than milk, and interacted with the beautiful children around the compound. We sat with the missionary families and learned about their mission work. It was challenging but life changing for our children and us. We were stretched, but it was a really good stretching and to this day Guatemala can still surface in conversation as a good family memory. However, we haven't eaten rice and beans as a family since that week.

THE SIX MOST IMPORTANT WORDS IN MARRIAGE

This chapter is titled, "The Six Most Important Words" and we need to get to those six words as we close this book. You've said them, but we also know they are the six most difficult words to say. It doesn't seem reasonable that they come with such difficulty, but they do. It doesn't seem rational for these six words to be so problematic, but they are.

What gets in the way of these words? A very simple but lifelong inhibitor—*pride*. Our pride can keep us from humbling ourselves. Our pride can hold us back from confessing that we are wrong or at the least our attitude is or was wrong. Pride, saving face, is what sin-filled humanness is full of. It's what keeps us defending ourselves when what we really need to do is confess our faults to one another and pray for one another (see James 5:16).

Proverbs tells us that pride goes before a fall or destruction (see Prov. 16:18). We can actually trip over our pride in our desire to somehow preserve our image before our spouse. But why? We know each other; we really know each other. For what purpose do I/we see pride serving me/us? Seriously, how has pride served you except to get you into trouble? There simply is no good outcome with pride-filled responses and attitudes.

Steve asked me (Mary) out of the blue one day why I can never apologize to him. I was aghast, appalled, and defensive. I asked him what he meant by that question in a very defensive tone of voice. He said, "You cannot apologize to me. You apologize to the kids and to others, but not to me." I really had to think about that for a while, and in conclusion I had to swallow my pride and admit that he was right. But I was baffled as to why I found it so difficult to apologize to the love of my life, my husband. Then, the Lord began to speak.

My father and mother raised eight kids. They loved us and provided well for our family. My parents were loving Christians and we were secure in their love and acceptance. There was an issue, though, with my father—he could not apologize to us kids if he wronged us. Sometimes he would discipline the wrong son or daughter, but he never apologized; he made it up to you. He won you over with his humor and his love. Somehow, my father's generation found it difficult to apologize, and I seemed to walk in a similar path of pride.

Do not hear me wrong—I am not blaming my inability to apologize on my father. It is my issue and I had to take responsibility for it. I was not going to blame him or use him as an excuse for my behavior; I was a grown woman. I had a conversation with God about my need to change and then something took place with my dad on a weekend in the mountains of Pennsylvania.

Our family was staying at a cabin with my parents. Our children were still pretty young. Our oldest son wanted to "help" his grandpa complete a work project, but he was only getting in the way. I was upstairs and I soon heard my father snap at my son. It brought back memories of my childhood, hearing that stern voice. I was ready to go intervene for my son when I felt the Lord stop me and say, "No, just wait. I'm at work here."

I heard the cabin door slap the jamb, and I watched my son with his head down crying while headed to the creek. I stood there in pain for my son. And then I heard the door slap the old wooden door jamb a second time. This time it was my father walking over to the creek where he thought my son might be.

Later that night when we were reading stories and putting our children to bed, I asked my son what grandpa said to him when he went and found him crying at the creek. He looked at me and said, "Grandpa apologized to me...for hurting my feelings...he said he knew that I just wanted to help and he was sorry."

I asked, "He said the words *I'm sorry*?" My father was changing. I knew then that I could change too.

Apologizing is still not easy, but I am using the six most important words with my husband now. Sometimes I say it jokingly, but I really do mean those words; they are so freeing, so liberating. Every married couple needs to incorporate them into their marriage and their family. It will bring healing and freedom.

THOSE WORDS...

What are the six most important words in marriage? Are you ready to hear them? Once you hear them, you will be accountable for knowing the right thing to say and to do.

I am sorry; I was wrong.

And, if you want to go a step further you can add three more words—*please forgive me.*

There you have it—the freedom of an apology. The goal is not to be right; it's to be in relationship—a healthy, whole, forgiving, amazing, loving relationship.

We invite you to go for many more amazing decades together. Young love is truly awesome, but old love is so rewarding and fulfilling. Stay together and enjoy a lifetime affair called marriage.

See Appendix C for an outline to the process of forgiveness.

PORNOGRAPHY AND SEXUAL ADDICTION RESOURCE LIST

BOOKS:

The Secret in the Pew: Pornography in the Lives of Christian Men by David A. Blythe

The author draws from his own story from his battle with sexual sin to provide a practical guide built upon God's Word to help others learn how to gain victory.

Facing the Shadow by Patrick Carnes, PhD

This workbook takes techniques used by thousands of people recovering from sex addiction and shows, in a step-by-step manner, how to break free of this disease and live a healthier, more fulfilling life. Each of this hope-filled work's chapters sets the stage for the recovery tasks at hand before providing practical, easy-to-follow exercises specifically designed to help readers understand and address them. Topics covered include why denial is so powerful and what can be done to counter it, how to face the consequences of behavior using recovery principles, how to respond to change and crisis, how to manage life without dysfunctional behavior, and how spirituality and recovery are interwoven.

This is not a Christian model of recovery but can be very effective if used side by side with scriptural principles.

The Way of Purity: Enjoying Lasting Freedom in Christ by Mike Cleveland

This workbook is a printed form of the online course from *Setting Captives Free* (which is no longer available). It provides a solid biblical framework to guide someone struggling with sexual sin to freedom in Christ.

At the Altar of Sexual Idolatry by Steve Gallagher

This book takes a closer look at the attitude of the heart in relation to sexual sin and provides a good resource rooted in Scripture pointing those suffering to the hope of Christ.

To Kill a Lion by Bruce Lengeman

Written by a professional counselor to counselors and strugglers alike, this book provides insight into the root causes of this sin in a person's life and provides solid biblical insights to help them achieve freedom.

The Pornography Trap: Setting Pastors and Laypersons Free from Sexual Addiction by Ralph H. Earle Jr. and Mark R. Laaser

This book is written to address the issue of sexual sin among pastors and laypersons serving in the church. The authors provide insight related to when leaders struggle and provide a guide to developing a biblical view of healthy sexuality.

Healing the Wounds of Sexual Addiction by Dr. Mark R. Laaser

This book by Dr. Mark Laaser traces the roots of the problem of sexual addiction, discusses the impact, yet provides a biblical approach to self-control and sexual integrity. This book is essential in helping one uncover the root causes of their acting out in sexual brokenness.

Seven Desires by Mark and Debbie Laaser

In this book, Mark and Debbie Laaser explore the seven desires given by God—to be heard, affirmed, blessed, safe, touched, chosen, and included. Using testimonies, a strong biblical foundation, as well as psychological principles, the Laasers provide an explanation of each desire, how to seek after it in a healthy way, and what each one looks like when it is truly fulfilled.

Shattered Vows: Hope and Healing for Women Who Have Been Sexually Betrayed by Debra Laaser

This book is written to the wives whose husbands have succumbed to sexual sin through pornography and sexual acting out. Drawing from her personal story of betrayal as well as her experience of helping thousands of other women, Debra Laaser provides practical tools to empower those who have been devastated by their husband's sin.

Storm Tossed: How a U.S. Serviceman Won the Battle of Sex Addiction by Jake Porter

Written under the pseudonym Jake Porter, this book is the testimony of a naval sailor who was sexually addicted from reading pornographic magazines, which led to acting out with prostitutes during his time in the military. The author found freedom through the power of Christ.

MINISTRIES:

Day Seven Ministries

Offers individual counseling and group support for men and women in sexual conflict over sexual abuse, sexual addiction, or homosexuality. Locations: Lancaster, Camp Hill, and Reading Pennsylvania.

Celebrate Recovery

According to the Celebrate Recovery website, "Celebrate Recovery is a biblical and balanced program that helps us overcome our hurts, hang-ups, and habits. It is based on the actual words of Jesus rather than psychological theory. Twenty years ago, Saddleback Church launched Celebrate Recovery with 43 people. It was designed as a program to help those struggling with hurts, habits, and hang-ups by showing them the loving power of Jesus Christ through a recovery process. Celebrate Recovery has helped more than 17,000 people at Saddleback, attracting over 70 percent of its members from outside the church. Eighty-five percent of the people who go through the program stay with the church and nearly half serve as church volunteers. Celebrate Recovery is now in over 20,000 churches worldwide! Go to www.celebraterecovery.com to find a group near you."

WEBSITES:

Fight the New Drug, www.fightthenewdrug.org.

This site raises awareness on the effects of pornography and provides links to the Fortify program, which is an online recovery program developed by them. This is not a Christian organization but does provide useful information on the damaging effects of pornography use on the brain, relationships, and the connection of pornography with the dark world of human sex trafficking.

Annual Marriage Evaluation and Vision Retreat

As you and your spouse walk through this process, create a document on which you will record your co-mission statement, scriptures, goals, and any other information. We recommend that you print this document and keep it in your Bibles for a quick reference to review and to pray over.

During this time, don't forget to enjoy your time away, go out for a nice meal, or see a movie together!

A. *Prayer*

Praying together as a couple is a key to this time:

- Start by giving thanks for God's provision from this past year.

- Pray about your time together during this retreat.

- Pray over your marriage, your family, your employment, your finances, etc.

- Give God praise for the positive and the not-so-positive.

- Assess your prayer lives together as a couple and as a family.

B. *Finances*

Take time to review your budget from the prior year:

- Where was your budget accurate? Where did it miss the mark?

- Review each of your banking accounts.

- Review your giving (tithe, missions, firstfruits, and offerings).

- Review your investments, such as life insurance, money market savings, retirement funds, etc.

- Review your debt and your plan to get out of debt. Are you in agreement with your debt and payment plans?

- Are you in agreement with your spending, credit card charges, and investments?

- Are you putting enough away for emergencies and retirement?

- How are you handling your children's educational goals?

- Are you meeting your financial goals in all of the above areas?

C. *Employment*

Review and evaluate your year of employment:

- Are you still called to this job or business?

- Are you meeting your financial obligations through this employment?

- Is there a possible change to your employment?

- Is there a side business you have or are interested in creating?
- What are your employment dreams?

D. *Schedules*

Review your activity level from the past year:

- Were you gone from home too often with employment or hobbies?
- Did you enjoy a sufficient number of dates with each other and your children? Did you have weekends away together? Did your family take a vacation?
- Assess your children's activities and your schedules.
- Share your anticipated schedules for the coming year. Project time away together. Project this evaluation time for next year.

E. *Vision/Goals*

Review your goals from the previous year:

- Review your marriage mission statement and make any necessary changes.
- Review any scriptures that you had recorded from the past year.
- Write your new goals and vision (spiritual, financial, social, emotional, mental, and physical).
- Create some goals that are beyond your resources and dream for the future.

F. *Life Strategies*

- Do you have any other life concerns that you need wisdom for?
- Are you caring for elderly parents?

- Discuss community connections for your family.

- Discuss your local church connections and vision.

- Discuss roles and duties in the home that you share or perform individually.

- Discuss any necessary diet changes and exercise routines.

- Discuss any other extraordinary concerns that you need to examine and pray through.

G. *Children*

- Discuss and evaluate your children's sports/extra-curricular activities.

- Discuss which school(s) they will attend.

- Discuss and plan your family vacation.

- Pray about and discuss any and all needs of your children or grandchildren.

- Discuss your need for family meetings to share important information with your children and to receive their feedback.

- Talk about your family devotional time. Are your children learning to pray and love God's Word?

- Pray through your family commitment to your local church and small group attendance.

- Candidly discuss as a couple and as individuals your quality and quantity time with your children.

- Discuss your disciplinary roles of your children. Is one parent doing more of the discipline? Do you need to switch roles at times so your children can identify your father's heart or mother's heart?

THE FORGIVENESS PROCESS

Jesus taught us in Matthew 6:14-15 that if we forgive others, the Lord will forgive us. You choose whether or not to forgive. As someone appropriately said, forgiveness is God's medicine. You will feel at times that the person who has angered you does not deserve forgiveness. Jesus did not say to forgive only those who deserve forgiveness. Forgiveness releases you, as well as the one who wronged you.

Forgiveness is an important ingredient in a marriage. Anyone in close relationship with another will encounter times of stress and frustration. It is at these times that we may say the wrong thing or behave in the wrong way. The following is a practical, step-by-step, scripturally based process for forgiveness.

This exercise completes the formal postmarital training. However, it is our hope that you will continue accountability, prayer, Bible study, and an ongoing desire to grow in your relationship with Christ and with each other. God bless you in your call together.

SEVEN STEPS TO FORGIVENESS

Anger can be a legitimate response. After the reaction of anger has been dealt with, we can then move toward forgiveness.

1. *Choose to Forgive.*

Forgiveness begins with a simple decision that, in Jesus' name, we will obey God and forgive those who have hurt us:

> And be kind to one another, tenderhearted, forgiving one another, even as God in Christ forgave you (Ephesians 4:32).

Jesus made it clear in Matthew 18:35 that this decision to forgive is to be from the heart. We are to forgive wholeheartedly, not holding back or keeping any resentment.

But what about feelings? Here are some helps in dealing with them.

- Forgiveness starts not with feelings, but with a decision. You don't need to wait for the right feeling before deciding to forgive. Instead, you can forgive! You can choose to forgive from your heart, and God will recognize that. Verbalize this decision: by faith confess aloud, "In Jesus' name I forgive _____." When you have done this, your feelings will be moving toward a resolve.

- Be alert! Satan may try to bring some feelings of resentment back into your life (see 1 Pet. 5:8-10). You do not need to feel guilty about these temptations, but you do need to deal with them. Since you have already made your choice, you need to stand firm on having already forgiven that person in Jesus' name.

- When that feeling of resentment comes back, say to yourself, "I did forgive! I dealt with that." Eventually when you remember that sad experience, it will be with the happy thought, "That's all over." Herein lies the healing of memories.

2. Confess Your Sin to God.

Unforgiveness is sin against God. It is disobedience to His command to forgive others even as God has forgiven us (see Eph. 4:32). Even more, God desires for all people to know forgiveness; He sent His Son, Jesus, to die to make that possible. Unforgiveness can stop people from experiencing God's forgiveness. Unforgiveness is a sin against God.

Yet God is always ready to forgive those who call on Him (see Ps. 86:5). So accept your unforgiveness as sin, and confess it to God. Do you know what He does then?

"If we confess our sins, He is faithful and just to forgive us our sins and to cleanse us from all unrighteousness" (1 John 1:9 NKJV). This confessing implies naming our sins one by one.

> He who covers his sins will not prosper, but whoever confesses and forsakes them will have mercy (Proverbs 28:13 NKJV).

How can we be sure we are forgiven? It's by God's Word! He very clearly says; For if you forgive men their trespasses, your heavenly Father will also forgive you (Matt. 6:14 NKJV).

Yet sometimes you still doubt that you are really forgiven. There is one more thing that you need to do. Receive God's forgiveness, accepting it just as you would accept a gift someone gave to you. How is this possible? Listen to what the apostle Paul said:

> Now then, we are ambassadors for Christ, as though God were pleading through us; we implore you on Christ's behalf, be reconciled to God. For He made Him who knew no sin to be sin for us, that we might become the righteousness of God in Him (2 Corinthians 5:20-21 NKJV).

3. *Ask Forgiveness From Those You Wronged.*

We are responsible to restore relationship with anyone who has anything against us (see Matt. 5:23-24). Accept responsibility for the wrong you have done, and ask for the person's forgiveness. If you do not know what you did wrong, ask God to show you.

Simply ask forgiveness. Do not go into details that would do more harm than good.

If you do not have a genuine sorrow or repentance in going to that person, stop first and prayerfully ask God to show you how you hurt that person and how they may have felt. Allow God to give you a whole new understanding and sensitivity toward that person.

It is good to look right at the person when you tell him what you did wrong and ask, "Will you forgive me?" Wait for an answer. If they say, "Yes, I will forgive," this will bring a release to them also. (Regardless of the answer, by confessing your sin and asking forgiveness, you have been obedient. You can now leave the situation in God's hands.)

4. *Ask God to Bless the Person Who Hurt You.*

> *Bless those who curse you, and pray for those who spitefully use you* (Luke 6:28 NKJV).

Ask God to truly bless the person who hurt you. And as you do this, follow the example of Jesus in asking God to bless him by forgiving him!

5. *Do Something Nice for the Person Who Hurt You (Bless Them).*

> *Do good to those who hate you* (Luke 6:27 NKJV).

> *Do not be overcome by evil, but overcome evil with good* (Romans 12:21 NKJV).

This could be accomplished by complimenting that person, baking some cookies, fixing their car, or babysitting. Ask God, and He will show some act that will be meaningful to that person.

6. *Accept the Person the Way They Are, Even if They Are Wrong.*

Do not defend what they do, but defend them. You do not necessarily need to approve of what they are doing, but treat them with dignity, respect, love, and kindness anyway.

> *Therefore receive one another, just as Christ also received us, to the glory of God* (Romans 15:7 NKJV).

7. *Look at the Person Through the Eyes of Faith.*

Do not concentrate on areas of weakness, sin, or irritation. Rather, concentrate on seeing that person as God wants him to be. Believe that God will answer your prayers for that person (see 1 John 5:14-15). Follow Abraham's example, and by faith see things that are not as they appear (see Rom. 4:16-21). Begin to think and speak positively about that person (see 1 Cor. 13:7). Love "believes all things, hopes all things."

SUMMARY

Here is a short, personalized summary of these seven steps to forgiveness:

1. In Jesus' name, I choose to forgive those who have hurt me.

2. I will confess my sins to God, especially the sin of unforgiveness. (And, by faith, I will receive God's forgiveness and cleansing.)

3. I will, as God directs me, ask others for forgiveness for the wrongs I have done to them. (And I will make restitution as needed.)

4. From now on, I will ask God to bless the one who has hurt me.

5. I, too, will bless that person, doing kind, helpful things for him.

6. I will accept him and treat him with love and respect.

7. I will look at that person through eyes of faith, and trust God to work in him.

List below any persons that you know you need to forgive. This list may include your spouse, a parent, a friend, a coworker, someone from your childhood, yourself, or perhaps even God.

_____

_____

_____

_____

_____

_____

_____

_____

Pray over this list individually or with your spouse and be accountable. Be sure to look back over the seven steps and see if you have completed them for each person you need to forgive.

About the Authors

STEVE and MARY PROKOPCHAK have been married for more than 40 years and have served as marriage and family counselors for much of that time. Their first book, *Called Together,* is an interactive workbook that has helped thousands of engaged couples from all over the world build a lasting marriage foundation. Steve and Mary have three adult children and two grandchildren, and they reside in Elizabethtown, Pennsylvania.

FREE E-BOOKS?
YES, PLEASE!

Get **FREE** and deeply discounted **Christian books** for your **e-reader** delivered to your inbox **every week!**

IT'S SIMPLE!

VISIT lovetoreadclub.com

SUBSCRIBE by entering your email address

RECEIVE free and discounted e-book offers and inspiring articles delivered to your inbox every week!

Unsubscribe at any time.

SUBSCRIBE NOW!

LOVE TO READ CLUB

visit **LOVETOREADCLUB.COM** ▶

www.ingramcontent.com/pod-product-compliance
Lightning Source LLC
Chambersburg PA
CBHW060756100426
42813CB00004B/836

* 9 7 8 0 7 6 8 4 1 6 3 8 1 *